D1470301

ALL-AMERICAN BOY

Discovering AMERICA

Mark Crispin Miller, Series Editor

This series begins with a startling premise—that even now, more than two hundred years since its founding, America remains a largely undiscovered country with much of its amazing story yet to be told. In these books, some of America's foremost historians and cultural critics bring to light episodes in our nation's history that have never been explored. They offer fresh takes on events and people we thought we knew well and draw unexpected connections that deepen our understanding of our national character.

Larzer Ziff

ALL-
AMERICAN
BOY

University of Texas Press

AUSTIN

Requests for permission to reproduce material from this work should
be sent to:
    Permissions
    University of Texas Press
    P.O. Box 7819
    Austin, TX 78713-7819
    www.utexas.edu/utpress/about/bpermission.html

All images except those from *Tom Sawyer* and *Huckleberry Finn*, which
are taken from modern reprints of the first editions, are reproduced
from first editions in the collections of the Sheridan Libraries, Johns
Hopkins University.

♾ The paper used in this book meets the minimum requirements of
ANSI/NISO Z39.48-1992 (R1997) (Permanence of Paper).

LIBRARY OF CONGRESS CATALOGING-IN-PUBLICATION DATA

Ziff, Larzer, 1927–
    All-American boy / by Larzer Ziff. — 1st ed.
        p.   cm. — (Discovering America ; 4)
    Includes index.
    ISBN 978-0-292-73892-8 (cloth : alk. paper)
    1. American literature—History and criticism.   2. Boys in literature.
I. Title.
    PS374.B69Z54   2012
    813'.009352341—dc23

                                                    2012017373

*In memory of
my brother "Morty"
(Howard Morton Ziff),
the boy I knew best.*

≡ CONTENTS ≡

ALL-AMERICAN BOY

≡ INTRODUCTION ≡

Webster's *Third International Dictionary* defines the term "all-American" as "thought of as representative of the U.S. as a whole." The example of usage that follows, "a real all-American boy," applies to the content of this book, which is concerned with the changing character of the all-American boy from his celebrated appearance, hatchet in hand, in Parson Mason Locke Weems's *Life of Washington* (1800) to Booth Tarkington's Penrod, who first appeared in 1914, reappeared in sequels, and then in the following decades was duplicated in many fictional boys in print and film who followed the pattern he had established.

Washington, who was ten when his father died, grew up to lead a revolution against the paternal authority of a king. His fellow Americans filled the resulting void by calling him the father of his country. It is, then, of some significance that despite the changes in the character of the all-American boy over the course of the nineteenth century, all save one were fatherless. Peck's bad boy is the exception, but an exception that, indeed, proves the rule, because the pranks that make up each episode of his adventures are aimed at discomfiting his father. Inasmuch as the boy in his person signaled a coming social change, freedom from paternal authority seemed an all but essential qualification for this role. But Penrod, the twentieth-century all-American who concludes this history, had a mother, father, and sister, and his mischievous escapades were, accordingly, cropped to conform to the conventions of middle-class, mid-American urban life. In outline he was the last of the all-American boys, but in substance he was the first of the new boys, members of traditional families, who later went on to enjoy popularity on screens as well as in books.

The popularity of each of the succession of boys who will be encountered here is one indication that their readers believed, or wished to believe, that the fictional boys were just like the boys they knew (or were), and one of the principal issues pursued in the following pages is that of the relation of these fictitious boys to the reality of their historical moment. Literary history, even a brief one such as this, is, inescapably, cultural history as well, and in many instances it is a consideration of the life of the author that enables me to move between the literary work and a sense of the social environment at the time it was written. In some cases, surprisingly few actually, the boy's fictional adventures are elaborated versions of the author's own experiences. But even though writing about a child, however fictitiously, inevitably involves drawing upon one's own childhood, the principal interest that the author's life claims in this history is not as an autobiographical source for the fiction, but as a register of social conditions at the time the fictional boy made his appearance, and of the contemporary issues that the author addressed in creating him. A literary work is not the result of social change; it is a participant in the process.

Jacob Abbott, for example, the author of the powerfully influential series of Rollo books, begun in 1835, was a college professor who left that career to pursue his interest in the relation of pedagogy to what was later to be called child psychology, founding both a progressive girls school and then one for boys in which the common practice of corporal punishment was banned and an honor system instituted, if not, indeed, invented. Although he was an ordained minister, Abbott occupied a pulpit for only a few years, preferring rather to concentrate on his experiments in pedagogy and then, increasingly, on his writing. At the age of thirty-two he retired from his activities in Boston and New York and returned to his hometown in Maine. Settling there, he concentrated on his writing, producing some two hundred books on history, theology, and current affairs, as well as several series of children's books, among them the twenty-four Rollo stories that served both as readers for children and manuals on child-rearing for parents. At play, in school, busy about the house, Rollo's mistakes, successes, and uncertainties were characteristic of the experience of boys of his age, although when the mischievous boy of a later age came to define the all-American boy, the name "Rollo" rather unjustly came in common parlance to mean a namby-pamby little gentleman.

No more exact opposite to Rollo and his America could be imagined than Hennery, the bad boy of *Peck's Bad Boy and His Pa* (1883), who rose to fame in the last decades of the nineteenth century. His gleefully sadistic pranks, aimed not only at his father, but also at other adult members of his society from preachers to organ grinders, were widely enjoyed in their day. Given their cruelty, one might well be led to account for the enthusiastic public reception they received by assuming that their appeal was to readers of the coarsest taste, which if proved true would be rather discouraging, since there were so many readers who followed them as they appeared serially in the newspaper in which they first appeared and then purchased the books into which they were collected. If, however, the career of George Peck, Hennery's creator, is brought into focus, another dimension is discerned. A Democrat, Peck was elected mayor of Milwaukee and then governor of Wisconsin in the decades following the Civil War, when the Republican Party, with its attendant social pieties and mounting financial corruptions, held national sway. In this context, Hennery's assault upon prevailing views of acceptable behavior begins to take on the form of deliberate social protest. It was a form of dissent, akin on the popular level to the literary attack on the conventions of small-town, mid-American life that were soon to appear in the stories and novels written by the more literary sons of the Middle West such as Edgar Lee Masters and Sinclair Lewis.

The changes in the character and behavior of the all-American boys in the procession that follows reflect changes in social attitudes over time. Tom Sawyer, for example, succeeds Rollo, risk-taking boy replacing dutiful son in successive periods. Yet great as their differences seem, each in his day was on his way to becoming the kind of responsible member the society of his adult years required. But other boys who differed from one another radically were actually contemporaries, and the popularity each enjoyed points to social and political divisions within the same society. In 1883, Peck's bad boy, for example, stood in pointed opposition to what Little Lord Fauntleroy would come to represent three years later when Frances Hodgson Burnett clearly aimed at Peck's boy in her narrative. Their differences were not sequential, but contemporaneous, each opposed to the other in the day's cultural struggles between vernacular, working-class Democrats and educated middle-class Republicans.

While a consideration of the lives of the authors in what follows contributes importantly to an appreciation of the historical reality that fictional boys from Rollo to Penrod entered, when appropriate I have also brought contemporary social documents to bear upon the subject. The transition from provincial Tom Sawyer to urban Ragged Dick and other Horatio Alger boys adrift on the streets of New York, for example, is accompanied by a consideration of the social analyses of Alger's friend Charles Loring Brace, an urban reformer. Or, in another instance, the late-nineteenth-century arrival of the concept of adolescence—previously the development from boyhood to adulthood had been thought of as without a distinctly different intermediate stage—brings the work of G. Stanley Hall, adolescence's "discoverer," into these pages. The recognition of adolescence, which separated teens from adulthood, essentially prolonged the period of boyhood and, consequently, produced the need both for school days to continue past the elementary grades and for the out-of-school activities of those now in the higher grades to be supervised. In this environment team sports assumed a widening importance, with the consequent ascension of the athlete as public hero that was captured in pulp fiction by Frank Merriwell, who never lost a game. His popularity is looked at in connection with the real-life career of Walter Camp, inventor of American football and creator of the first "All-American team."

· · · · ·

The principal figures in Chapter 1 are the young George Washington created by Parson Weems in 1800, and Rollo, who followed him some thirty years later to illustrate the characteristic experiences of boyhood in an American village. Washington's youth was spent in a colonial society that observed the law of primogeniture, with its consequent emphasis upon paternal authority. Writing in the newly independent United States, Weems shied away from dealing with this social structure to emphasize instead the moral bond that existed between father and son regardless of social conventions. Three decades later, however, in his Rollo books, Jacob Abbott was dealing with the young citizen of a republic and what was to be expected of him. Political independence did not in itself negate the doctrine of infant damnation, which continued in force in large segments of the population, and in preparing his boy for adult life in the United States, Abbott had to confront and reform educational practices still based on that doctrine.

Chapter 2 commences with Thomas Bailey Aldrich's *Story of a Bad Boy* (1870), in which the mischievous yet good-hearted, disobedient yet responsible boy, occupant of a reality apart from that of his parents, arrives to replace the good boy as the all-American boy. This "bad boy" was the product of two worlds, that of the pre–Civil War America of the narrative and the postwar America of its author. Without the accelerating culture of economic competition in the latter period, the boy's mischievousness in the former period would not have been celebrated. Now it could be regarded as a promising prelude to business success. Tom Sawyer, who arrived in 1876 to become the iconic all-American boy, clearly owed a good deal to Aldrich's bad boy, but in his shorter writings before *Tom Sawyer*, Mark Twain had already written a number of pieces about boys, including one with "Good Boy" and another with "Bad Boy" in the title, and these pieces are resurrected and discussed before *Tom Sawyer* is brought forward.

Chapter 3 turns to the boys of urbanizing America in the latter decades of the nineteenth century, with a glance in passing at farm boys, none of whom, curiously, came to be valued as all-American despite the fact that for more than a century the United States was a nation of farms. A discussion of Horatio Alger's heroes—or, perhaps, hero, since he was the same figure under many names—is followed by considerations of Peck's bad boy and Burnett's little lord, who was born and raised in modest circumstances in New York City before leaving for England to teach republican good manners to his grandfather, the Duke of Dorincourt. Of great significance in this literary period is that each of the boys, which is to say each of their authors, was well aware of the others and what they stood for, and Peck's Hennery, Alger's Ragged Dick, and Burnett's little Cedric engage in implicit, and on several occasions explicit, exchanges with one another.

Chapter 4 begins with the recognition of adolescence in the last decades of the nineteenth century and the consequent extension of required schooling and the separation of classroom groups by age. The all-American boys in their previous incarnations had been fatherless—even Frank Merriwell, the ever-triumphant sports hero, was being raised by an absent uncle—but with the appearance of Booth Tarkington's Penrod the household environment changed. He had a father, a mother, and a sister, and while he too was fertile in mischiefs, his world, nevertheless, was now defined by family, class, and also race, upon which Tarkington expended a surprising amount of attention. His influence upon popular culture from his day through to the end of the twentieth century was great. Unlike his predecessors, Penrod was destined to grow up to be just like his father, and with him to be American came to mean to be white, middle-class, and, culturally, mid-American.

The concluding chapter considers the two boys who stand as definitive antitheses to the all-American boy and thus define him by contrast: Huckleberry Finn and Holden Caulfield. Huck, as the title page of his novel proclaims, was Tom Sawyer's "companion." But Holden, who arrives a half-century after Penrod, is not the companion of any Tom Sawyer of his day, but rather a critical opponent of any such contemporary, his presence a strong indication that the day, indeed even the concept, of the all-American boy had definitively passed.

Washington portrait opposite title page of Weems's Life.

≡ THE NEW NATION ≡

Young Washington, Rollo

George Washington first chopped down the cherry tree in 1806, seven years after his death. There is no mention of that incident in the first edition of *The Life of Washington*, by Parson Mason L. Weems, published in 1800, the year after Washington's death. But, as Weems subsequently wrote to his publisher, Mathew Carey, "You have a great deal of money lying in the bones of old George,"[1] and Carey arranged an enlarged edition of the *Life*, which appeared in 1806. In this and all subsequent editions, young George wielded his hatchet. Henry Cabot Lodge, who in 1889 published a scholarly biography of Washington, observed that nine-tenths of the content of Weems's book was drawn from the newssheets of the day and was known to everybody, while the remaining tenth, which described Washington's boyhood, was the exclusive product of Weems's imagination. But this tenth, of course, is the part that has lived on in American legend. Weems was from Maryland and knew the Mt. Vernon region and its inhabitants well. Accordingly, at those places in which he exercised his imagination in order to describe Washington's childhood, he said that he was repeating what old people who had known Washington as a boy had told him.

Ordained an Episcopal priest in 1784, Parson Weems served successively in two Maryland parishes until 1792, after which time he never again became attached to a single living, although he continued to preach in one or another church along the border between Maryland and Virginia. But after marrying in 1795 he sought to support his family by working as a traveling book agent for Mathew Carey of Philadelphia, in which occupation he sold Bibles, and books, and tracts, some of which he himself had written. Weems knew his potential buyers needed assurance that they were contributing to the moral and spiritual betterment of their families before they invested in a commodity so apart from their material needs as a book, and in the early pages of his *Washington* he emphasized the uplifting moral influence the book would have upon children. The title page exhorted:

Lisp, lisp his name, ye children yet unborn!
And with like deeds your own great names adorn.

And in the opening chapter he explained, "Since then it is the private virtues that lay the foundations of all human excellence—since it was these that exalted Washington to be '*Columbia's first* and *greatest Son*,' be it our first care to present these, in all their lustre, before the admiring eyes of our *children*."

When dealing with his publisher, however, Weems assumed another tone. Pressing Carey to follow up the *Life* with a collection he would prepare, to be called *Beauties of Washington*, he said that a panegyric on the title page would read:

George Washington Esqr. The Guardian Angel
of his Country
Go thy way old George. Die when thou wilt
We shall never look upon thy like again.

Perhaps Carey's reluctance to go through with that project stemmed from his recollecting the speech in Part One of Shakespeare's *Henry IV*, in which Falstaff, unaware that his cowardice at Gadshill had been witnessed by Prince Hal, apostrophized himself as the last, living exemplar of true manhood: "Go thy ways, old Jack, die when thou wilt; if manhood, good manhood be not forgot upon the face of the earth, then am I a shotten herring." Placing Washington in even veiled proximity to Falstaff might have been too much for Carey. At any rate, the *Beauties* never appeared. As Marcus Cunliffe wrote of Weems, "There is a touch of the confidence man in him. That he sincerely loved Washington did not preclude his love for the profit in him, and in melding patriotism with profit he demonstrated his own Americanism." And, to be sure, there is actually something engaging in that!

· · · · ·

Visiting the United States in 1836–1837, Alexis de Tocqueville noted the rapidity with which sons in a democratic society became independent of their fathers, in contrast to their continued dependency in aristocratic societies, where primogeniture played a defining role: "As soon as the young American begins to approach man's estate the reins of filial obedience are slackened."[2] Previously, in America's colonial period, family life did closely replicate the patriarchal pattern of the English homeland. In Puritan New England, for example, a father directed his son's life until the youth reached manhood, seeing that he was not only well behaved but also well instructed, which is to say drilled and taught to believe what he was to think for himself when he reached the age of discretion.[3] He was responsible for placing his son before he was fifteen in a suitable apprenticeship, where he was to serve until he earned independence at the age of twenty-one. In his *Autobiography*, for example, Benjamin Franklin recalled that when he was twelve he was sometimes taken by his father on a walk "to see Joiners, Bricklayers, Braziers, &c. at their Work, that he might observe my Inclination, & endeavor to fix it on some trade."[4]

Although their social patterns were very different from those of the New England family, among the members of George Washington's social class in colonial Virginia the father's role as mentor and disciplinarian was equally strong. "Never did the wise Ulysses take more pains with his beloved Telemachus than did Mr. Washington with George," Weems wrote. Although Augustine Washington may not have believed, as did the Puritan parent, that all children were subjects of God's wrath unless catechized in the way of salvation, he did not hesitate to admonish his son with a biblical fervor:

> Truth, George, (said he) "is the loveliest quality of youth. I would ride fifty miles, my son, to see the little boy whose heart is so *honest*, and his lips so *pure*, that we may depend on every word he says. O how lovely does such a child appear in the eyes of every body! His parents doat on him; his relations glory in him; they are constantly praising him to their children, whom they beg to imitate him. They are often sending for him, to visit them; and receive him, when he comes, with as much joy as if he were a little angel, come to set pretty examples to their children."

After which he described the opposite case of the boy who lied and was looked at with aversion wherever he went. "Oh George! My son! rather than see you come to this pass dear as you are to my heart, gladly would I assist to nail you up in your little coffin, and follow you to your grave." With this grim warning firmly in place, the cherry tree anecdote, "too valuable to be lost, and too true to be doubted," follows.

For the modern reader, adult as well as boy, the obnoxious child in the examples Augustine Washington spelled out for his son is not so much the little liar as the boy whose behavior is so angelic that he is constantly held up to less seraphic children as a model to be imitated—nay, is even invited into their homes to set them an example then and there—to show them up, as it were, by comparison. Should this little angel have paid his exemplary visit anytime after, say, 1850, he would, at the very least, have received a well-deserved kick in the shins from his juvenile hosts. But in Weems's day and before, as well as in Freud's day and after, the strongly held, nigh universal belief was that, as Milton phrased the matter, "The childhood shows the man/As morning shows the day," and Weems constructed the boy in terms of the virtues he intended to show in the man. Writing in the vituperative atmosphere of slanderous accusations that marked the 1800 presidential contest between the supporters of Adams and those of Jefferson, Weems singled out devotion to truth as Washington's cardinal virtue. And, notably, in view of Washington's military achievements, he also pictured a Washington who abhorred boyish combativeness and dutifully cooperated with adult suppression of such behavior.

After the death of his father, Weems writes, George, at the age of ten, was sent to live with his half brother in Westmoreland in order to attend a school there. Popular with his fellow students, he was a leader in their games. He used to divide his playmates into two armies, "and every day, at play-time, with corn-stalks for muskets, and calabashes for drums, the two armies would come out, and march, and counter-march, and file off or fight their mimic battles, with great fury." But so far was this from revealing a streak of militancy in young George that although the other boys actually fought one another in earnest, "he was never guilty of so brutish a practice as of fighting himself, nor would he, when able to prevent it, allow them to fight one another. If he could not disarm their savage passions by his argument, he would instantly go to the master, and inform him of their barbarous intentions." In so doing, he violated what even in his day was a cardinal principle in the boyhood code: he informed on his fellows, or, as the act would have been termed in the slang of his day, he "squeaked" on them. Moreover, he did so with full knowledge of how they would regard his action. But, according to Weems's supposed informant, "a very aged gentleman" who had been a schoolmate of George's, George would say, "angry or not angry, you shall never, boys, have my consent to a practice so shocking! shocking even in *slaves* and *dogs*; then how utterly scandalous in little boys at school, who ought to look on one another as brothers." He then painted them a picture of tender parents who see their child returning from school with black eyes and bloody clothes like a common blackguard, simply to win the praise of other boys. Imagine the parents' feelings! "Big boys, of the *vulgar sort*, indeed may praise him: but it is only as they would a silly game cock, that fights for their *pastime*."

Washington was, Weems wrote, "born to be a soldier," yet for Weems the progression from boyhood abhorrence of fighting to adult leadership in war was coherent. George's summoning the master to interfere when his own persuasion failed to prevail with his peers revealed a respect for, and dependence upon, paternal authority that he had learned at his father's knee and that he himself would come to rely upon as father of his country.

The American Revolution may have dispatched a king, but for some decades into the nineteenth century, social as opposed to political forms remained similar to those that had existed in colonial days. With boys increasingly moving outward geographically in order to move upward economically, paternal rule was steadily loosening, as Tocqueville noted in 1836. Yet any clear sense of its replacement, of, that is, the nature of a new family order appropriate to life in a republic, was slow to emerge. For more than fifty years after the publication of the *Life*, the young Washington that Weems invented inhabited popular culture as the ideal American boy.

Abraham Lincoln told his biographers, Nicolay and Hay, that as a boy he had read Benjamin Franklin's *Autobiography* and enjoyed it, but it was Weems's *Washington* that "stirred his imagination." Although that youthful Washington is remembered today only because he could not tell a lie, the other model deeds dramatized by Weems, especially those that emphasized submission to paternal authority, also formed part of what Americans in the first half of the nineteenth century held to be praiseworthy boyhood behavior.

· · · · ·

In his study of campaign biographies, William Burlie Brown noted that the ideal of happy youth in the period from 1844 to 1868 was "a model child, interested neither in pranks nor in athletics." Before 1844, the boyhood of the candidates was not deemed a necessary part of the biography, and Brown conjectured "the relatively youthless candidates of the pre-1844 biographies indicate by their silence the widespread belief that the ideal youth was one who was 'seen and not heard.'"[5] Only after 1868 was the boy who would be president mischievous and full of pranks. Before then, he was ideal because well behaved, even gentle, considerate of his fellows, and respectful of authority. This is certainly evident in the biography Nathaniel Hawthorne composed in 1852 for the presidential campaign of his friend Franklin Pierce. As did Washington's, so Pierce's father filled his son's world to its horizon. Franklin Pierce's father, Benjamin, had served in the Revolution, was general of his county's militia, and was later elected governor of New Hampshire. "From infancy upward," Hawthorne wrote, "the boy had before his eyes, as the model on which he might instinctively form himself, one of the best specimens of sterling New England character developed in a life of simple habits yet of elevated action. He became early imbued, too, with the military spirit which the old soldier had retained from his long service, and which was kept active by the constant alarms and warlike preparations of the first twelve years of the present century."[6] But that "military spirit" was possessed by a boy with extraordinarily mild manners. As Weems had done, so Hawthorne relied upon "old people" who had known his subject as a boy to provide information about that period of his life (but his sources seem to possess more substance than Weems's shadowy informants). They told Hawthorne that Franklin was "a beautiful boy, with blue eyes, light curling hair, and a sweet expression of face. The traits presented of him," Hawthorne continued, "indicate moral symmetry, kindliness, and a delicate texture of sentiment." In a glimpse of things to come, Hawthorne was perhaps a bit uneasy with this portrait of a gentle boy, because he went on to assure prospective voters that "the boy did not show the germ of all that was in the man." Still, he saw no need to suppress evidence of the boy's endearingly sweet disposition, and given Pierce's electoral victories, he was not alone in believing that such gentleness foreshadowed the kind of manliness required of one who would lead a nation.

The most striking aspect of the similarity between Weems's and Hawthorne's biographies lies not, however, in what they said, but what they did not say. In both accounts the boys' mothers take little or no part in directing their sons' conduct. When ten-year-old George's father died, his mother took immediate steps to place him under male supervision, and authorial praise for his gentleness, a quality associated with women, could be read as praise for his acceptance of paternal guidance, and the same may be said of Hawthorne's Pierce, although his mother was not widowed. He was instructed, not reasoned with.

As, however, the last generation of postrevolutionary parents who had been born in colonial America passed away, with them adherence to a pattern of family government that reflected the autocracy of colonial political government also faded away. Then reason, the sanctified foundation of civic life in the new republic, broke through into domestic life as well. The emerging form of republican family governance assumed a son who had to be reasoned with rather than commanded, not only to convince him of the correctness of what was expected of him, but because the well-being of a republican society as a whole depended upon his being trained in the exercise of his reason. This responsibility extended to his mother, who entered the conversation to represent father and son to one another. A model of how this new kind of family conducted itself influentially emerged in the series of Rollo books that began appearing in 1832 and served as both entertaining stories and manuals of behavior for tens of thousands of American families. At the age of seventy, Henry James, looking back at his own childhood reading, spoke affectionately of the "sweet" Rollo series that sounded the note of New England and "determined a shy yearning" in his expatriated boyhood.[7] The Rollo books were also among the volumes in his personal collection that Bernard Berenson donated to the Harvard University library.

· · · · ·

In 1835, T. H. Carter, a Boston book agent, approached Jacob Abbott, minister of the Eliot Congregational Church in Roxbury, with a proposition. He had on hand twenty-four engravings that he wished to publish in book form, but the subjects depicted in the engravings were rather scattered: a bear with a nose ring led by an organ grinder, a man crossing the ice on foot, a boy and girl with a bow and arrow, a dog, another dog in water, a butterfly, three different bird pictures, not to mention a girl feeding birds, a number of other animal pictures, a garden, flowers, and boys playing with fire (or was it exploding gunpowder?). Could Abbott supply him with a text that would somehow lead from one picture to the next so as to justify their inclusion in a single book?

Having been involved in publishing earlier works by him, Carter knew his man. Abbott was the author of *The Young Christian*, a serial in four volumes that had had an immediate success upon its publication in 1832 and had been published in French and Dutch translations in addition to having been published in England. He agreed to undertake the commission, and in that same year *Rollo Learning to Talk* appeared, with a text that asked the child to whom the book was to be read to point to the parts of the picture that were being discussed, a precursor of what would come to be called "interactive learning." Carter paid Abbott $150 for writing the book, which concluded with the lines: "This is the end of little Rollo's Picture Book. Who do you think little Rollo is? I will tell you all about him in the next book."

Up to that final point, however, the name "Rollo" had not appeared in the text. The book began, "These little talks about pictures are mainly intended to be read by a mother, or by one of the older children, to a little one who is learning to talk." But by the end, Abbott clearly had that "little one" in focus and so gave him a name and promised his reappearance, which, indeed, was to occur in plenty. *Rollo Learning to Talk* became the first of twenty-six Rollo books that were, in effect, as much manuals on child development as children's books. Rollo grew from babyhood to the age of ten or so in a series of exemplary stories that children could read on their own, even as the narratives introduced parents, especially mothers, to principles of child-rearing that were more liberal, or, as one would later call them, more "child-oriented," than those that prevailed when Rollo made his first appearance.

The books in the Rollo series went on to be published and republished by printers in Boston, Philadelphia, New York, and elsewhere well into the twentieth century. Everyone knew the name Rollo, even those who were not among the thousands upon thousands who had read the books, and "Rollo" became a synonym for a well-behaved little boy. He continued to be so well-known a cultural figure that in the Roaring Twenties of jazz and gin rickeys, the satirist George Chappell (author of *Through the Alimentary Canal with Gun and Camera* and *The Gardener's Friend and Other Pests*) was able to produce *Rollo in Society, a Guide for Youth*, knowing that his readers would be familiar with the subject of his satire. In it he not only introduced young Rollo to wine, women, and song, but did so by carefully mimicking Abbott's prose, confident that readers, beyond thinking of the properly brought-up child when they heard the name "Rollo," would also have some familiarity with the style in which the Rollo books were written if they were to savor the satire fully.

In the American as in the English tradition, the primary aim of education was held to be moral rather than intellectual, and like Weems's *Washington* and the selections in the McGuffey Eclectic Readers, widely used in American schools, the Rollo books also placed moral education at the fore. But in addition, unlike similar schoolbooks and children's tales, the Rollo stories placed an unprecedented emphasis upon the boy as a rational being who even at an early age was capable of understanding distinctions finer than good or bad, right or wrong. Miss Mary, Rollo's first schoolteacher, for example, can explain to her class: "When you do wrong, your guilt depends upon your heart, your intentions, and your acts, and not upon the bad consequences that follow. When bad consequences follow, they do not make you guilty when you mean and do right; and if they do not follow, that does not make you innocent when you mean and do wrong." The children thus come to understand why one member of their class who "did wrong" has been punished, while another has not. Rollo is asked to think, not just to obey.

• • • • •

Rollo's creator, Jacob Abbott (1803–1879), was born in Hallowell, Maine, where his father was a merchant. At the age of fourteen he passed the entrance examination for Bowdoin College and was admitted to the sophomore class. He earned his bachelor's degree in 1820 and was awarded the master's degree in 1823. For several years after leaving Bowdoin he taught at Portland Academy. Longfellow, who was one of his students, later recalled that he was "very amiable and indulgent and much beloved by his pupils."[8] In the fall of 1821, Abbott entered Andover Theological Seminary to prepare for ordination as a minister in the Congregational Church, completing that training in 1824, but instead of entering immediately upon a ministerial career, in that year he accepted a tutorship in mathematics and natural philosophy at Amherst College, and one year later was appointed to a professorship.

In the year of Abbott's arrival, Amherst College was but three years old, still very much in the process of defining itself. He became the leading spirit in a group of five young faculty members who were conducting research into the methods of other colleges and universities in Europe as well as America, and at the annual meeting of the college's trustees in 1826, he presented the group's findings. Affirming that Amherst's curriculum was not "sufficiently modern and comprehensive,"[9] he urged a more liberal course of study in which French and German were substituted for Latin and Greek, and emphasis was placed on modern history and science. The trustees agreed to this recommendation being incorporated into a parallel course that students who wished could elect instead of the traditional course, but, in the end, tradition and precedent proved too much for the parallel course:

> Only a handful of undergraduates registered for it in the autumn of 1828, and the Trustees, in the following summer, voted to abandon it. Professor Abbott, disgruntled and disillusioned, resigned at this meeting, with the knowledge

that his cherished experiment had failed. If it had received the full and enthusiastic support of his colleagues, it might conceivably have made Amherst a pioneer in the educational world. As it was, it left no residuum, except a permanent course in French.[10]

One further incident at Amherst serves to fill out the picture of Abbott as a nascent reformer of both education itself and the notions of child psychology on which it was based. During his stay at Amherst, he was put in charge of the college's buildings and grounds, for which office he received an extra fee. While he served in that position, the old wooden tower in which the college bell was located was under his charge. When one day the boy whose duty it was to ring the bell summoning the students to daily prayers reported to him that the key to the tower had been stolen, Abbott told him to knock off one of the slats of the structure, gain entry, and ring the bell. The boy did so, and when he asked what he should next do Abbott told him to leave the opening as it was and go off to his recitations. So long as the slat remained off and entry to the tower presented no challenge to other students, the bell remained undisturbed. And so when construction of the new chapel had been completed and the bell was installed there, Abbott advised the faculty not to lock the chapel door. He was overruled, the chapel was keyed, and student pranks, such as the removal of the bell's clapper, resumed.

Leaving Amherst, Abbott took charge of the newly founded Mt. Vernon Young Ladies Seminary in Boston, where he famously instituted—in effect invented—what in later years and at many other institutions became known as the "honor system," under which the students themselves governed conduct; this in a day when corporal punishment was the usual consequence of misbehavior in school. When Abbott was asked what punishment he would apply to those who violated the system, he answered, characteristically, by drawing a distinction: there would be no punishment, but there would be consequences.[11]

In 1834 Abbott was named minister of the newly founded Eliot Congregational Church in Roxbury, but increasingly interested in devoting his time to writing the juvenile literature for which he was acquiring a wide reputation, in the following year he turned his pulpit over to his brother John and moved his family to Farmington, Maine.[12] He was not, however, through as yet with practicing his reforms in schools, as well as promoting them on the page, and he briefly conducted a school for boys in Boston, modeled on the girls' school he had administered there, and then with two of his brothers founded another school, the Abbott Institute, in New York City. Finally, in 1851, he returned home to Farmington, residing there and devoting himself to his writing for the remaining twenty-eight years of his highly productive life.

A complete list of Abbott books, notably but far from exclusively in juvenile literature, consists of more than two hundred titles. In addition to the Rollo books, for which he is principally remembered today, he produced a number of other series, such as the "Franconia Stories" and the "Lucy Books." When the editors of *Harper's Monthly Magazine* decided to make the burgeoning American industrial scene an important part of each issue, the first piece published on the theme was Abbott's account of the Novelty Iron Works in New York City. He wrote a series of history books designed for a general readership that Harper's marketed as the Red Histories, and shortly before his death Abraham Lincoln wrote to the publisher about them:

> I have not education enough to appreciate the profound works of voluminous historians; and if I had, I have no time to read them. But your series of Histories gave me, in brief compass, just that knowledge of great men and events which I need. I have read them with great interest.

To them I am indebted for about all the historical knowledge I possess.[13]

The Andover Seminary Abbott and his brothers had attended was established in the first decade of the nineteenth century in reaction to the drift away from Calvinist orthodoxy that the Seminary's founders saw occurring at the Harvard Divinity School, a drift which, along one path, led to Unitarianism and then beyond that to Transcendentalism. But although an Andover man, Abbott's educational reforms arose from his adoption of a liberal theology.[14] In his America, educational practice was based upon religious belief. "In the first half of the nineteenth century," Abbott's son Lyman wrote, "the more or less deliberate purpose of religious parents in Puritan households was the government of children by fear of a tyranny which could not be resisted and the suppression by that government of the natural instincts of childhood."[15] Such practice stemmed from the theology of an inherent depraved nature—"In Adam's fall sinned we all"—with the consequence that the child needed to be subdued. "My father abhorred controversies of every description and never attacked the current theology of the time," Lyman Abbott continued, "but all his children's books were based upon a psychological conception radically different."[16]

Viewing Abbott's Christian children's writings, then well known in England, John Henry Newman chided that he came near to promoting Socinianism, the doctrine of the denial of the divinity of Jesus, and in this regard Abbott had indeed come close to Emerson's exposition of the humanity of Jesus in his famous 1838 address to the Harvard Divinity School. Seeking to turn ministers away from reiterations of doctrine in the face of a silent congregation, Emerson had also insisted, "Truly speaking, it is not instruction but provocation that I can receive from another soul." Abbott's ideas of childhood education ran parallel. Children should be inspired

23

to question and experiment, not simply be treated as empty vessels in need of instructional stuffing.

During Abbott's own childhood, the port of Hallowell, where his father had his business, was second only to Portland as the busiest place in the District of Maine, its wharves receiving goods directly from the West Indies, with sixteen stage lines centered in the town to carry passengers and freight inland. Hallowell was part of the wider world and, intentionally or not, imported ideas together with cargoes of rum and molasses. Abbott's wife, Helen Vaughan, a native of Hallowell, corresponded with Mary Peabody of Salem, sister of Elizabeth, Emerson's amanuensis, and of Sophia, who was to marry Hawthorne. Moving back to Maine, the Abbotts nevertheless continued to be part of the great cultural tide that was to be labeled the "American Renaissance." At Farmington, Abbott purchased property across from his childhood home and built a house on it. Thereafter he spent half of a typical day at his writing table and the other half outdoors, working on his land. The writings, which earned him a comfortable living, depended upon his being culturally as well as commercially connected to the nation. If for him writing was a form of business, a principal part of it was the elaboration of the American child's ability to think. In the preface to *The Little Philosopher*, one of Abbott's earliest works, little William asks, "'What is Philosophy, mother?' She answers, 'It is the first thing which children learn.'"

• • • • •

Rollo has a father, a mother, and a little sister. They live, one may surmise from their routines, in a small town in New England. An older boy, Jonas, who works as a handyman in the garden and fields surrounding their home, also lives with the family. Part of his business is to take care of Rollo. He shows him how to do the tasks Rollo has set for himself,

Jonas takes Rollo to his first day at Miss Mary's school.

for example, how to use a wheelbarrow instead of a basket to transport firewood, and how to make his own playthings: form a whistle out of a reed, or shape a wigwam by leaning branches against a tree. While Jonas supervises Rollo's behavior in practical matters, more complex aspects of behavior, such as the governing of one's desires or the need to deliberate before acting, are supervised by his parents. Once Rollo is old enough to attend school—on the first day Jonas walks along with him to see that he doesn't loiter, but on subsequent days he goes by himself—Miss Mary, the teacher, also participates in his moral education, dealing principally with the social questions that arise from his and the other children's first experience of spending extended periods of time with their peers rather than at home with adults.

Considered out of their context, the number of verbal corrections Rollo receives from these combined supervisors might look staggering, but they are absorbed into the larger narrative of the activities of a happy child who likes his home and likes his school. The strong assurance he acquires in these settings provides him with the capacity to assimilate, and even on occasion to welcome, criticism. Moreover, so far as young readers are concerned, when Rollo falls into need for correction, he does so because he has done something they are able to recognize that they themselves have done. A comparison of the correction he receives with their own experience can claim their interest.

One day, an eagerly anticipated outing to pick blueberries had to be canceled because of rain. Rollo was disappointed and he began to sulk. He returned time and again to talking of his disappointment and so persisted in this that his father finally stepped in to tell him that his behavior was "self-conceited, ungrateful, undutiful, unjust, selfish, and even impious," after which he spelled out for him the separate connotation of each of those six adjectives. Next, Rollo's mother advised him that when one is disappointed in pleasure, the best thing is not to seek another pleasure but to turn to some duty. For readers in a later day, the sum of these corrections can appear to have a weight disproportionate to Rollo's offense, yet if they are placed on one tray of a scale opposite the tray that bears the *New England Primer*'s affirmation of infant depravity, or Augustine Washington's assurance that he would sooner nail little George up in his coffin than learn that he had lied, the tray on which Rollo's corrections are placed flies up in the balance.

Rollo's socialization in school also takes place under supervision, but contains as well a large component of objective information. Dovey, who had a knife handle but no blade, gave Rollo, who had a blade but no handle, her handle. When he returned to school with the blade inserted into the handle, Dovey argued that he should return her handle to her in its present form, while he argued that she had given him the handle yesterday and that it was now his. In a separate incident, Julius had seized George's paper windmill and refused to return it.

Miss Mary, the teacher, holds court. The windmill case is clearly one of robbery, the definition of which she supplies, and the windmill must be restored to its owner. But the matter of the knife and its handle is more complex. "When a person gives or sells any property," she explains, "it is called a conveyance. If this is done under such circumstances, and in such a manner as to make the thing fully and fairly the property of the person who receives it, it is called a *valid* conveyance." What, then, are the conditions that make a conveyance valid? First, Miss Mary explains, the property must be owned by the person who gives it, so that she has a right to convey it. Next, she must have intended to convey it, that is, give it away entirely, not just lend it. And, finally, she must actually deliver it to complete the conveyance:

> For example, if a boy were to promise you a whistle and say he should bring it the next day, and then the next day should bring it and refuse to give it to you, you would have no right to take it. His promise to give it to you would not make it yours. It is necessary that he should actually deliver it to you of his own accord. Now these are the rules men observe and I think they apply to children as well.

Miss Mary's elaboration of legal distinctions is a sterling example of Abbott's reliance on the intellectual curiosity of children and his confidence in their reasoning ability. Wanting something back after it has been given to another is a feeling the children in her class recognize, and Miss Mary's explanation engrosses their attention. It clears things up for them, and Abbott's assumption that young readers, with their experience of "Indian giving," would also follow the rules of conveyance with interest seems sound as well as original. The appeal to the intellect of children convincingly on display in this passage is typical of the approach in all of the Rollo books. Given their popularity, it may safely be assumed that such passages were not read as humdrum interruptions of "the story," but held considerable interest in their own right.

· · · · ·

Yet Rollo's exemplary ability to respond to reason is not only the means by which he may discover his own identity, but also the way in which society enlists him into its service, and it functions with an effectiveness at least equal, if not superior, to the earlier pattern of patriarchal insistence upon obedience. Consider, for example, Rollo's situation on the day the sun does shine and the postponed blueberry expedition takes place. While in the field he is drawn to the hill where some boys are already picking and the berries seem more plentiful. His father had earlier warned him not to go near those boys, but the attraction of the plentiful berries, and also, one can well suspect, the attraction of freedom from restraint that the unattended boys represent, lead him to join them, whereupon the boys proceed to tease him, spill the berries he had already picked, and throw him to the ground. When he returns in outraged tears to his family, he complains about how unfairly he had been treated. But his father points out that the fault lies with him for disregarding the paternal warning, and that he should be penitent about that rather than place the blame for what happened upon others. "I did not positively command you not to go near the boys, or not to have any conversation with them at all, though I expressed my wish that you would not, so that you could not help to understand it," his father says. The distinction thus drawn between a wish that Rollo could not but understand and an actual command seems, in the context of the penitence required of Rollo, somewhat duplicitous, a granting of free will only insofar as the recipient exercises it as the grantor expects him to, but it is preparation for an adult recognition of the limits a free society places on the action of its members. They may stray beyond what is advised into what is not actually forbidden, but in so doing they have no right to redress should they come a cropper.

The subtitle of *Rollo at Work* is *The Way to Be Industrious,* and when the six-year-old becomes bored quickly with a chore he has undertaken and leaves it, his father explains that "it is very necessary that you should have the power of confining yourself steadily to single employment, even if it does not amuse you. I have to do that, and all people have to do it, and you must learn to do it, or you would grow up indolent and useless." Such paternal advice goes a long way toward explaining why later in the century the spirited adventures of Tom Sawyer, who came to be idealized as the archetypical American boy, were enabled by his being fatherless.

As the difference between understanding a paternal wish, which Rollo is expected to do, and obeying a paternal command, as boys in an earlier day were expected to do, begins to blur in practice, so, too, does the difference between an earlier age's belief in infant damnation and the more liberal views of childhood failings held by the adults who supervised Rollo's development. "Now a school," says Miss Mary, "is in some respects like a hospital. Children are sent here partly to be cured of their faults and improved in character. If any children have bad characters they may be said to be morally diseased or sick, and I want to cure them."

Abbott's emphasis upon the intelligence of children is praiseworthy. It bestows upon them a wholeness that earlier educational theory repressed. But when it reached a crucial crossroad, it halted. Rollo and his classmates ask whether it is wrong to ask adults "Why?" Some tell Miss Mary that when they do ask their parents "Why?" they are told not to do so, while others say when they ask their question is answered. She asks for examples, and then explains. When Rollo asks his father why the toy raft he built does not float, he is right to do so. It expresses a desire for knowledge and deserves the explanation it receives. But to ask "Why must I go to bed?" when told to do so is wrong; it is simply an excuse for not obeying. Yet why is that not a legitimate question that also deserves to be addressed, although it is not? The implicit answer would seem to be that children should adjust their conduct to the greater good of the family—and, by extension, of society.

· · · · ·

I f, as previously noted, Abbott's views on educational psychology resembled Emerson's, and, more generally, his writings moved along the same stream that propelled the major works of the American Renaissance, it is also necessary to note his divergence from Emerson's deep-running current into a more tranquil mainstream. "A boy is in the parlor what the pit is in the playhouse," Emerson wrote in "Self-Reliance," "independent, irresponsible, looking out from his corner on such people and facts as pass by, he tries and sentences them on their merits, in the swift summary way of boys, as good, bad, interesting, silly, eloquent, troublesome. He cumbers himself never about consequences, about interests, he gives an independent genuine verdict." But such behavior, Emerson recognized, does not comport with the demands of society, which are everywhere "in conspiracy against the manhood of every one of its members," and press the boy into compliance. Consequently, Emerson insisted, "Whoso would be a man must be a nonconformist."

For Abbott, however, a democratic society has equitable demands to make upon its individual members, and Rollo's moral education is also an education in social responsibility, in, that is, participation in a democratic society. He is a model boy. He is also, in his rational compliances, close to being the opposite of the all-American boy who will succeed him.

≡ ALL-AMERICANS ≡

Tom Bailey, Tom Sawyer

In the early months of 1869, *The Story of a Bad Boy* by Thomas Bailey Aldrich was published serially in *Our Young Folks*. It was an immediate success. Before the final installment appeared, the juvenile magazine had added several thousand readers to its list of subscribers, and after its publication in book form later that year (although it bore the date 1870) Aldrich's autobiographical novel "speedily ran through some eleven editions, a notable record for a book of its kind in those days."[1] Before Aldrich's book, boy stories written in America had assumed a readership composed almost exclusively of boys, and this, joined to the conscientious belief that children's books must offer a picture of children behaving in accordance with what adults deemed best for them, resulted in an abundance of stories about young milksops that seemed to have been written by grown-up milksops. It surely occurred to adults who read such stories that their own childhood was not at all like that of the model children they encountered there, but that memory did not suggest to them that it was either proper or valuable to represent boy life as it really was. Of course, boys did not behave as well-mannered adults, but literature's role in guiding them to that end was to place ideal models before them.

Such a didactic view of children's literature was a facet of a larger belief, widely shared in pragmatic America, that the office of literary fiction in general was to present to the reader the social world as it should be rather than as it was. As late as 1897, the highly successful novelist F. Marion Crawford would still argue, "Let us sometimes talk about men and women who are unimaginably perfect, and let us find out what they would do with the troubles that make sinners of us."[2] The same belief in the instructive rewards of fiction had from colonial times governed the depiction of the impossibly good, or his converse, the truly wicked, boy.

In the aftermath of the Civil War, however, the principles and practice of literary realism, already prominent in European, especially French, fiction, began to take hold in the United States. Its great exponent, both as critic and novelist, was William Dean Howells, who in his review of *The Story of a Bad Boy* in the *Atlantic Monthly* of January 1870 wrote: "No one else seems to have thought of telling the story of a boy's life with so great a desire to show what a boy's life is, and with so little purpose of teaching what it should be; certainly no one else had thought of doing this for the American boy." What Howells could not then but suspect was that Aldrich's success would be followed by an impressive number of American writers, himself included, turning to their own boyhood as subject for their books, most notably Mark Twain, the adventures of whose Tom Sawyer were to resemble in a number of ways those of Aldrich's Tom Bailey. While Aldrich's novel is, as his biographer characterized it, "a *composed* picture of vivid memories," in which "the sequence of events bears little or no relation to the chronology of its author's own boyish life,"[3] Twain's is, in the main, made up of imagined incidents rooted in a recollected past. Notable boyhood books by others, such as Charles Dudley Warner and Hamlin

Garland, are closer to a sequence of actual events and might be called autobiographies.

Pondering the outpouring of books about boys written as much for an adult as a juvenile audience, Van Wyck Brooks conjectured that in the "somewhat inglorious postwar epoch, boyhood seemed better than manhood. At least, the leading authors wrote about it with a relish they seldom brought to the rest of life."[4] His suggestion resonates. The realism Howells saw Aldrich applying to the portrait of the American boy was to be the mode of authors who were looking back upon a boyhood separated from them not only by their age but by a cataclysmic war that they had to look past in order to bring their subject into focus. They needed, that is, to reconstruct a political world that no longer existed, as well as the life of the boy who inhabited it, and the success of their narratives is closely tied to the extent to which they were able to bring antebellum town, hamlet, or farmstead back to life.

In the most celebrated English novels of the century, Charles Dickens had dealt extensively with the boyhood of his eponymous characters such as Nicholas Nickleby, Oliver Twist, and David Copperfield, but then carried them into the adulthoods that arose from their earlier experiences. But *The Story of a Bad Boy* and the other adult narratives of American boyhood that followed in its wake were entirely devoted to that stage of life and came to a close when boyhood ended. The Civil War, an event unforeseen by any character in these books, had opened an historical abyss between boy and man much wider than that which time alone could have opened. The prewar world of their boyhood stood by itself. It was, in both senses of the word, *finished,* ended yet complete, and this condition made it possible to visualize the life of a boy in that period as, in the same way, finished, independent of whatever adult emerged after the war.

· · · · ·

Born in Portsmouth, New Hampshire, in 1836, Thomas Bailey Aldrich spent the first three years of his life traveling with his family as his father sought business opportunities in one or another part of the United States before settling in New York. Then after another three years the family again moved, this time to New Orleans, where Aldrich's father became part owner of a bank and where the boy appears to have enjoyed a number of happy years. New Englanders that they were, however, his family intended him for Harvard, and so when Tom was thirteen he was taken back to Portsmouth to live with his maternal grandfather and great-aunt so that he could attend a school that would prepare him for college more effectively than any in New Orleans. This Portsmouth is the Rivermouth in which the "bad boy" Tom Bailey has his adventures.

In the same year that Aldrich was deposited in Portsmouth, his father died of cholera while traveling down the Mississippi on business. Although not foreseen then or for several years thereafter, one consequence of this death was that when the boy neared the time for entry into Harvard his family was forced to recognize that his father's death had not left sufficient money to support him at college. Instead, it was arranged that he become a clerk in his uncle's countinghouse in New York.

Although he was perhaps disappointed, Aldrich does not appear to have been distraught at this change of fortune. He had published some of his early efforts at poetry in the Portsmouth newspaper, and in New York he was situated in a lively literary scene even as he continued to work in the countinghouse. When he proudly told his uncle that he had received fifteen dollars for a poem from an editor at *Harper's,* the reply was "Why don't you send the damned fool one every day?"[5] If Aldrich did not quite do that, he did, nevertheless, continue to write poems and send them out for publication, and also increasingly to participate in the activities of New

York's rather raffish literary community. He felt so well suited to that life that in 1859 he left the countinghouse to work for the *Saturday Press*, a magazine founded in the previous year that saw itself as the champion of Bohemian New York's assault upon the propriety of the eminent literati of Boston. But the year after Aldrich joined it, the *Saturday Press* folded, announcing in its final number, "This paper is discontinued for lack of funds, which is, by a coincidence, precisely the reason for which it was started." By the time of that demise, however, Aldrich was sufficiently known in literary circles in Boston as well as New York to be able to support himself by freelance writing and editing.

Ticknor and Fields, the leading literary publishing house in America, issued *The Poems of Thomas Bailey Aldrich* in 1865, and in 1866 Aldrich moved to Boston and went to work for that firm (soon to become Fields, Osgood, and Company) as editor of *Every Saturday*, a magazine made up, in the main, of articles taken from English and French periodicals, aimed at a readership that wished to retain (or acquire) a cosmopolitan sense. Since American law did not protect the copyright of foreign periodicals, the greater part of *Every Saturday* was, in effect, pirated.

Shortly after Aldrich settled into his new job, William Dean Howells arrived at the same house to serve as assistant editor of the *Atlantic Monthly*. They were soon close friends bantering about their respective positions: Aldrich's was, they agreed, more important because he was the editor of *Every Saturday*, but Howells's was more eminent because, although he was only an assistant editor, his magazine was the *Atlantic. Our Young Folks*, in which *The Story of a Bad Boy* first appeared, was also a publication of Fields, Osgood, and Company. It was edited by J. T. Trowbridge, whose stories and novels for children were widely read in that day, among them *Cudjo's Cave* (1864), an antislavery novel for children. Fields, Osgood, and Company was a nursery for America's fledgling writers, as well as the publisher of most of its eminent authors.

Aldrich, the onetime Bohemian, was to settle comfortably into Boston life, happily declaring that although not a Bostonian he was at least "Boston-plated." He assumed the editorship of the *Atlantic* in 1881, from which post he retired in 1890, after which he traveled to Europe several times and added travel writing to the poetry and fiction that he continued to publish throughout his life. In 1896 an eight-volume edition of his collected works appeared. If not as famous as Howells and Twain, who were in 1904 two of the seven founding members of the American Academy of Arts and Letters, he was, nevertheless, together with Henry Adams and Henry James in the group of eight elected in the following year. He died in 1907.

Aldrich's writing, Van Wyck Brooks wrote, "was undoubtedly distinguished. It was lucid, skillful, crisp and fresh, and the neat-handed Aldrich always knew when to stop, an unusual virtue."[6] Unlike the Westerners Howells and Twain, he was a wit rather than a humorist, very much a later century (and less highly wrought) version of Oliver Wendell Holmes, and this sharpness kept him from sentimentality when he reminisced about his boyhood. Mark Twain, who first met him in 1871—they were to remain friends for the remainder of Aldrich's life—called him the "wittiest man in seven centuries."[7]

In 1866, the year he moved to Boston, Aldrich wrote an enthusiastic letter to his friend and fellow poet Bayard Taylor, then in New York, about the cultural life he now saw opening before him:

> The people of Boston are full-blooded *readers*, appreciative, trained. The humblest man of letters has a position here which he doesn't have in New York. To be known as an able writer is to have the choicest society open to you.

Just as an officer in the Navy (providing he is a gentleman) is the social equal of anybody—so a knight of the quill here is supposed necessarily to be a gentleman. In New York— he is a Bohemian. Outside of his personal friends he has no standing.[8]

The letter thus speaks to his limits as well as his sense of arrival. By the time Aldrich entered it, Boston's literary society had descended into the twilight that followed the high noon of Emerson, Hawthorne, Holmes, Lowell, Longfellow, and Whittier. Significantly, Howells, responding to New York's obstreperous vitality and its checkerboard immigrant population, was to move there from Boston in 1889, but Aldrich, who would succeed him as editor of the *Atlantic*, remained in what became, in effect, a gated cultural community. While Emerson had believed that the tidal wave of immigrants from many lands and cultures would create a new American race—Whitman's teeming "nation of nations"— Aldrich came to speak of such immigrants as a "wild motley throng" that menaced the true America.[9]

Well into the twentieth century one or another poem or story by Aldrich found a place in anthologies of American literature. But although it is his best book, *The Story of a Bad Boy* did not keep pace and has disappeared from general circulation. In its day it was regarded as the equal of *Tom Sawyer*, and while that judgment now seems overblown, it is, nevertheless, closer to a measure of the book's strengths than is the disregard under which it has since suffered.

· · · · ·

"This is the story of a Bad Boy. Well, not such a very bad, but a pretty bad boy and I ought to know, for I am, or rather I was, that boy myself." With those sentences Thomas Bailey Aldrich begins a narrative that twenty-two chapters later concludes, "So ends the Story of a Bad Boy—but not such a very bad boy, as I told you to begin with." The rather coy tone of these remarks—not, thankfully, present in the narrative itself—is a clear signal that Aldrich wants his character to be read against the literary convention of the good boy as the model American boy. In the preface to an 1894 reprinting of the book he made this explicit, saying that he "wished simply to draw a line at the start between his hero—a natural, actual boy—and that unwholesome and altogether improbable little prig, which had hitherto been held up as an example to the young."

And, to be sure, Tom Bailey is not a bad boy in any meaningful moral sense. The misdemeanors he and his spirited companions commit are harmful neither in intent nor result, and the adults who, custom dictates, must punish escapades such as the setting off of nighttime explosions that wake the town or the purloining of a discarded old buggy to feed the July 4th bonfire are, at bottom, amused by them. They are reminded of their own youthful behavior, and the token punishments they administer are merely for form's sake.

In his survey of presidential campaign biographies, William Burlie Brown notes that between 1868 and 1900 the ideal happy youth ascribed to a candidate was that of "a mischievous child full of boyish deviltry, and fond of physical exercise and personal [as opposed to team] sports."[10] He ran, he swam, climbed trees, rode horses, and played tricks upon other boys and also, at times, upon adults. Aldrich wrote his book in the first of those framing years. His Tom Bailey kept stride with the impending presidency of Ulysses S. Grant.

Throughout the novel Aldrich speaks as an adult looking back on his own boyhood. Although this and the books like it that followed did not advance beyond boyhood, nevertheless an adult moment was always present in the voice of the narrator looking back at himself, and the many adult readers who took pleasure in these books did so in good part because they also were remembering their careless years. Boy readers, on the other hand, were absorbed in looking straight at what other boys had been doing.

Contrasting Tom's genteel childhood in New Orleans, where he was served by slaves and kicked "little black Sam" whenever anything upset him, with the life he entered upon in Rivermouth, Aldrich writes, "Daily contact with boys who had not been brought up as gently as I worked an immediate and in some respects a beneficial change in my character. I had the nonsense taken out of me, as the saying is—some of the nonsense at least. I became more self-reliant." Yet in the opening pages of the *Story* this observation is accompanied by the cheerfully offered observation that whenever a new student arrived at his school Tom would confront him, give his name, and ask the new boy his name. "If the name struck me favorably, I shook hands with the new pupil cordially, but if it did not, I would turn on my heel, for I was particular on this point." Just what "this point" was is left for the reader to infer from examples provided: "Such names as Higgins, Wiggins, and Spriggins were deadly affronts to my ear; while Langdon, Wallace, Blake, and the like, were passwords to my confidence and esteem." Remarkably, this annoying information is gratuitous insofar as the narrative that follows is concerned, because in it no Higginses or Wigginses or their like, presumably working-class Irish, put in an appearance in order to be scorned. The boyish "villains" are named Conway and Rodgers and are schoolmates who are held apart from Tom's society not because of their names but because they are bullies, they pick on smaller boys, and are sneaks, quick to inform on those responsible for one or another prank. If there is a trace of class prejudice in the novel, it may arise from the fact that Conway's mother is a dressmaker, while Tom's grandfather, who lives in a house the family has inhabited for nearly a century, is known in town as "Captain" because he held that appointment in the local militia during the War of

1812. We may, if we wish, see snobbery in this. But Aldrich brushes by such a possibility when with some delight he deflates the Captain's status by reporting that he never left home during his wartime service and the only exploit under his command was the farcical mistake of attacking a boatload of men, who were rowing ashore in the dark to seek water, in the belief that they were an invading army.

Tom Bailey lives neither on a farm nor in a big city. Farm boys are working boys without the leisure to be bad in the sense that Tom is bad, while the characteristic big city boy—Horatio Alger's *Ragged Dick* was published the year before *The Story of a Bad Boy*—was acutely aware of the proximate social class to which he did not belong and unwilling to jeopardize his desired entry into it by acting in a mischievous manner. All of which is to note that the rascally boy who replaced the gentle young George Washington and the innocent, teachable Rollo was a product of the middle-class American town. Outside of school his time was pretty much his own to use in play or the pursuit of other interests; his recreations were not managed by his elders. Only later in the century would clubs and institutions arise to organize and supervise boys' free time.

· · · · ·

Writing in a children's magazine in 1900, Theodore Roosevelt advised all boys to read *The Story of a Bad Boy* and *Tom Brown's School Days*. The latter book, by yet another Tom, Thomas Hughes, had been published in 1857 and continued to appear in edition after edition through the nineteenth and the following century. It was considered to be classic reading for boys, although one may suspect that like *Alice in Wonderland*, a much better book, it achieved that status because adults believed it was the kind of book children would like and so presented it to them, rather than because there is convincing evidence that children were delighted when they did read it. There was a large difference between the boarding school to which English Tom Brown went off before he was twelve years of age to spend the years until he reached young adulthood and the local school to which American Tom Bailey went off each morning and from which he returned home each afternoon at the end of the school day. But Aldrich clearly knew and admired Hughes's book. At the point in his *Story* that Tom Bailey must confront the bully Conway and have it out in fisticuffs (similar confrontations are a feature of many boy books), Aldrich addresses his young readers directly, enjoining them: "Learn to box, to ride, to pull an oar, and to swim," after which he quotes at length from *Tom Brown's School Days* to emphasize his point, especially the need to learn to box.

Tom Bailey fought Conway in order to stop him from pushing around a younger and smaller boy. As a consequence, from then on the defeated Conway stopped persecuting Tom's small friend and ceased taunting Tom himself. In his novel, however, Hughes had unfolded a grander vision of the beneficial consequences of knowing how to fight, elevating pugilistic proficiency from a private to an imperial obligation. "From the cradle to the grave," he tells *Tom Brown*'s readers, "fighting rightly understood is the business, the real business, honestest business, of every son of every man. Everyone who is worth his salt has his enemies, who must be beaten, be they evil thoughts and habits in himself or spiritual wickedness in high place, or Russian, or Border ruffians, or Bill, or Tom, or Harry, who will not let him live in quiet until he is thrashed." Although this peppy bellicosity may in some degree have accounted for Roosevelt's high regard for *Tom Brown's School Days* in the heady days of 1900 when the United States itself was well into its imperial venture, in 1868, Aldrich, with the memory of the Civil War strong upon him, wrote, "According to my thinking, the hospital teaches a better lesson than the battlefield. I will tell you about my black eye, and my swollen lip, if you will; but not a word of the fight."

The parallels between Hughes's and Aldrich's books serve, finally, to point up Anglo-American differences on the subject they have in common. While both deal with schoolboy life outside the classroom, in *Tom Brown's School Days* that extracurricular life is, nevertheless, also lived within the walls of the school itself, and, as Charlotte Mitchell writes, "Rugby School is England, and the experience of the boy, learning self-reliance so that authority may be delegated to him, symbolizes the experience of the man of the ruling class."[11] In Aldrich's novel, on the other hand, Tom leads his extracurricular life in the house of his grandfather and the town of Rivermouth. Insofar as we wish to assert that his experiences prepare him for adult responsibilities, those responsibilities are not so much constrained by what he owes to class and country as by what he owes to his own best self. As Mitchell observed, Tom Brown learns "self-reliance" so that "authority may be delegated to him." The self-reliance Tom Bailey is gaining, however, is not attached to class or country or any other responsibility, but more closely resembles what Emerson meant by the term in his essay "Self-Reliance," an independence of mind answerable to itself rather than society for the judgments it makes. A boy's forthrightness, Emerson said, is the "healthy attitude of human nature," which becomes lost in the conformity that society progressively requires of a boy as he grows older. His assertion challenged, by design, the doctrine of original sin and the consequent need to counter the depravity of human nature with instruction and punishment. To be natural is to be good, not sinful.

Sharing this belief, however, Aldrich in his novel nevertheless facetiously echoed the previous convention of what was good and what bad in order to illustrate its obsolescence by dramatizing just how bad the bad boy really wasn't. Social conservative that he was, he could hardly have been in agreement with Emerson's contention that "Society everywhere is in conspiracy against the manhood of every one of its members." But he was American enough to regard responsibility to self as prior to social duty, and bourgeois gentleman though he became, he nonetheless arrived there after he had forsaken the security of the countinghouse in answer to the inner voice that called him to the hazard of a life in letters.

Tom Brown's School Days begins with a splendid picture of village life in the Vale of the White Horse, where Tom was born. He is sent off to Rugby to learn, in effect, how to maintain that way of life by serving one or another of the institutions that preserve it. "Many is the brave heart," Hughes writes, "now doing its work and bearing its load in country curacies, London chambers, under the Indian sun, and in Australian towns and clearing, which looks back with fond and grateful memories to the schoolhouse drawing room, where much of the highest and best training was received." It was from extracurricular experiences such as those in the drawing room of the headmaster's wife, not in the classroom of the teachers, that the young learner derived a sense of correct manners and obligatory duties. On the day Tom Brown arrives at Rugby his stagecoach is met by a student of his age who hires one of the grown men lounging about to carry Tom's luggage up to the school for sixpence, adding with a self-assured air, "And hark'ee, it must be up in ten minutes or no more jobs from me." At that moment Tom Brown began his training as a member of the governing class.

Tom Bailey's schooling, on the other hand, is continuous with his life at home; he does not leave the private and go into the public world when he enters school, because the two worlds are already mingled. Each morning he leaves home to go to school, and each afternoon after school he returns home. If his school is restricted in the sense that it is attended only by boys whose families can afford to keep them off the labor market past the age of fifteen, it and its students are, nevertheless, very much part of the everyday life of the town. The boys' adult lives may very well take them away from their hometowns, but that is a feature of the American linkage of upward social mobility and outward geographical mobility, not of their explicit assumption of responsibilities to class or country. When Aldrich makes brief mention of the adult careers of Tom's boyhood friends, he does so with none of the rhetoric that elevated the labors of Hughes's curates, barristers, and plantation managers to the level of imperial service. Phil Adams, who always had a scanty head of hair, is now American consul in Shanghai—a shaved skull and long pigtail would very much suit him; "Pepper" Whitcomb, who received his nickname because of the abundance of freckles on his nose, although now a judge probably has spectacles perched on the bridge of that very same nose; Fred Langdon, who used to make the most delicious licorice water Tom ever tasted, is now in the wine business in California; and Jack Harris, who commanded their group in the annual snowball fight with a group of other boys, died leading a Union cavalry charge at the Battle of Seven Pines. Each is remembered with quiet amusement that what he became was very much like what he had been. But whether they became curates, or barristers, or plantation managers, Tom Brown's schoolmates knew that as adults they would be "bearing the load"; that is, in their individual careers they would also be taking up a share of the burden of empire. The self-reliance of the American boys served their nation only insofar as the aggregation of their personal achievements contributed to the well-being of the nation.

· · · · ·

"In America," Tocqueville had observed during his visit to the United States, 1831–1832, "there is in truth no adolescence. At the close of boyhood he is a man and begins to trace out his own path."[12] The majority of American boys began their working lives before or at the age of fifteen, and that, in effect, then made them adults. "As late as 1854," Joseph E. Kett writes in his invaluable history of the subject, "Roget's *Thesaurus* equated adolescence with 'being out of one's teens,' with manhood, virility and maturity—with everything, that is, but childhood and sexuality." The concept of adolescence, he says, was "the creation of a distinctive mind set, an expression of a mélange of nostalgia and anxiety, and in its crudest mold an embodiment of Victorian prejudice about females and sexuality."[13] Only after 1900 was adolescence in its modern sense recognized, one of its principal markers being the youthful struggle with sexuality in a society governed by an injunction against premarital sex.

It is not surprising, then, to find that throughout the nineteenth century American novels about boys that were aimed at an adult audience did not characterize boy-girl relations in terms other than what might be called "playing house"; that is, the two paired off in imitation of the apparently chaste domesticity of husbands and wives. Perhaps the most singular feature of *The Story of a Bad Boy*, however, is that this, the first of the bad boy novels, is also the only one to portray a moment of sexual arousal.

One day toward the end of summer, Nelly Glentworth, a nineteen-year-old cousin, arrives at the house to pay a visit of some days to her great-uncle and great-aunt. Tom, some five years her junior, is very soon in love with her, forsaking all opportunities to join his friends in one or another boyish activity in order to remain in her company. He does not describe Miss Nelly's figure in detail, referring only to her chestnut braids, her complexion, her height, voice, and smile, but he is clearly falling in love with a fully formed woman, as the adult Tom implies when he says that "the small boy experienced a strange sensation and mentally compared her with the loveliest of Miss Gibbs's young ladies and found these young ladies [schoolgirls of his age] wanting in the balance." He knows that the reason Nelly rumples his hair when she sees him, takes his hand when they are out walking, and leans over to kiss him when he has a headache is because she regards him as a little boy, and this realization torments him: "I was wretched away from her and only less wretched in her presence."

The narrating Aldrich doubts that Nelly knew the nature of Tom's passion until the evening before her departure, when the two sat in a darkening autumn room lit only by the flames in the fireplace. Conscious that this is his final opportunity to declare his love, Tom haltingly begins by asking whether she will remember her visit to the family after she leaves, and receiving a routinely polite answer, presses on to ask whether she loves anyone. Of course, she says, she loves their uncle and their aunt and him and Towser. "Towser, our new dog! I could not stand that." He jumps up from her side in anger: "That's not what I mean." What he wants to know, he insists, is whether she loves anyone well enough to marry him. "The idea of it," Nelly says, and laughs. But he demands that she must tell him, at which point, appearing perplexed, she gets up to leave. Tom grabs her dress, but she calls him silly, rumples his hair, and runs from the room laughing.

> I hesitated a second or two, and then rushed after Nelly just in time to run against Miss Abigail [his great-aunt], who entered the room with a couple of lighted candles.
>
> "Good gracious, Tom!" exclaimed Miss Abigail, "*are* you possessed?"
>
> I left her scraping the warm spermaceti from one of her thumbs.[14]

The diminuendo that follows Tom's evening with Nelly—she departs the next morning in company with the young man she will marry—is perfect in pitch, a witty recounting of the following days during which Tom's heartache modulates into an assiduous struggle to retain its languor even as it slips

46

away. He became, he says, a "blighted being." "It was a great comfort to be so perfectly miserable and yet not suffer any." "If I could have committed suicide without killing myself I should certainly have done so."

The novel closes with Tom's genuine grief at the news of his father's death and his departure from Rivermouth to take a place in his uncle's countinghouse in New York.

• • • • •

The event at which Thomas Bailey Aldrich and Mark Twain first met was a lunch held in Boston in honor of Bret Harte, who was in the city to give a reading. Twain, too, was in town to read, but in 1871 Harte was the more famous author. Regarded as a popular entertainer rather than a serious man of letters, Twain in his dress and deportment did little to contradict that perception. His trousers and jacket did not quite match one another either in color or pattern, and his vernacular speech was not what a literary man was expected to have. In part, these differences may have been deliberate. Audiences were buying tickets to hear the man who had written the jumping frog story, and if they expected a countrified westerner he would oblige them. But in truth he had come east from the mining camps of Nevada and California and without trying did stand out in bold relief against an urban setting. Indeed, when Aldrich, delighted by his new acquaintance, brought Twain home to dinner, his determinedly proper wife sat stonily silent, refusing to announce the meal until Twain took the point and departed, leaving Aldrich to endure her wrath at his having brought into their home a man whose careless dress and lazy drawl, she could only conclude, meant that he was drunk.

Mark Twain's rise to fame had begun in 1865 with the publication of his sketch "Jim Smiley's Jumping Frog" in the *Saturday Press* of New York.[15] The piece quickly caught the attention of newspaper editors in all regions of the country, who enthusiastically reprinted it, and within weeks the name of an obscure West Coast reporter was known nationally. The jumping frog story was the best, but only one, of the many sketches that Twain had been sending to magazines in the 1860s, and on its strength a number were gathered and published in 1867 as *The Celebrated Jumping Frog of Calaveras County, and Other Sketches*, Twain's first book.

The sketch "Story of a Bad Little Boy," which had been published in the *Californian* in 1865 (the same year that the jumping frog story made its first appearance), was also in the book. It was an unsubtle lampoon of the perfect good boy who was a leading character in the day's conventional Sunday-school books. In it, his opposite, the bad boy, does everything that the books guarantee will bring ruin down upon him, yet blithely remains unscathed. On Sabbaths he goes hunting but does not shoot off three or four of his fingers, goes fishing but is not struck by lightning, and goes swimming but does not drown. Worse still, when he steals the teacher's penknife and the good boy is accused of the theft, there is no kindly man who happened to be passing to witness the crime and step forth to exonerate the good boy. Instead he is punished for the bad boy's crime: "Everything about this boy was curious— everything turned out differently with him from the way it does to the bad Jameses in the books."

The parody is so predictably repetitious it would scarcely hold attention were it not for the irresistible voice of the narrator as he ambles with unimpeded ease down a road of compound sentences littered with the apparently superfluous details that actually serve the sketch's satiric intent more effectively than do the episodes themselves. So, for example, the observation that follows the bad boy's successful raid on an apple tree: "It was very strange—nothing like it ever happened in those mild little books with marbled backs and with pictures in them of men with swallow-tailed coats and bell-crowned hats, and pantaloons that are short in the legs, and women with the waists of their dresses under their arms and no hoops on." With such apparently clueless drifting into irrelevance, we already in 1865 are in the presence of Mark Twain and the emergence of an American style.

Clearly, Twain's bad little boy is a figure cut from cardboard just as are the good boys in the books that are being ridiculed. Twain was approaching *The Adventures of Tom Sawyer* (1876), but in 1870 was not yet finished with the simpler theme. In "Story of a Good Little Boy," published in the *Galaxy*, the outcome of one after another incident is again certain to be the reverse of what is preached, and again the attractive colloquial sentences meander along to unexpected pleasures at their close. "The good little boy knew it was not healthy to be good. He knew it was more fatal than consumption to be so supernaturally good as the boys in the books were, he knew that none of them had ever been able to stand it so long, and it pained him to think that if they put him in a book he wouldn't ever see it, or even if they did get the book out before he died it wouldn't be popular without any picture of his funeral in the back part of it." As one-dimensional as Twain's bad and good boys were, however, sparks of Tom Sawyer's coming adventures glimmer briefly in the bad boy's Sabbath conduct and the good boy's pain at the thought that he would not be present to witness his own funeral.

Another sketch, published in the *Galaxy* two months after the good boy sketch appeared there, is more ambiguous in its approach to exemplary behavior, as if between the sketch's start and its close Twain had changed his mind about its intent. In "The Late Benjamin Franklin," Franklin is at first parodied as someone whose simplest acts were contrived for the sole purpose of being held up for imitation by succeeding generations of suffering boys: "With a malevolence without parallel in history, he would work all day, and then sit up nights, and let on to be studying algebra by the light of a smouldering fire, so that all other boys might have to do that also, or else have Benjamin Franklin thrown up to them." Further examples drawn from Franklin's *Autobiography* are also caricatured, followed by parodies of Poor Richard's maxims. But as the joke thins and all but staggers to a halt, a long paragraph strikes another note. It begins soberly; "Benjamin Franklin did a great many notable things for his country, and made her young name to be honored in many lands as the mother of such a son." Then, almost in apology for the preceding burlesques, Twain says, "I merely desired to do away with somewhat of the prevalent calamitous ideas among heads of families that Franklin *acquired* his great genius by working for nothing, studying by moonlight and getting up in the night instead of waiting till morning like a Christian, and that this programme, rigidly inflicted, will make a Franklin of every father's fool. It is time these gentlemen were finding out these execrable eccentricities of instinct and conduct are only the *evidence* of genius, not the *creators* of it." This admonition pretty much reverses whatever fun may have been derived from the preceding parodies, although Twain seeks to recover their lightness with a characteristically anticlimactic close, saying that when he was a child he was forced to get up early "and study geometry at breakfast, and peddle my own poetry, and do everything just as Franklin did, in the solemn hope that I would be a Franklin some day. And here I am."

So there he was: in keeping with the sketch's theme presumably a failure, at least, far from a great man. Yet one cannot resist thinking forward from there to the Mark Twain who in books and platform appearances around the world became the most famous American of his day. Although it may be fatuous to assume that in 1870 Mark Twain foresaw this future, the uneasy flickering between satire and respect in the Benjamin Franklin sketch suggests that as he wrote the piece he, once a printer's apprentice, was coming to feel an identity with the printer's apprentice who rose to international renown, not despite his humble beginnings and distinctively American manner, but with the aid of them.

"Washington is the hero of great actions, Benjamin Franklin is the typical American writ large,"[16] Ruth Miller Elson observed in her study of nineteenth-century American schoolbooks. Among the more striking differences between the two as they figure in American legend is that Franklin by his own account was a bad boy. He led his childhood friends in filching stones from a building site in order to build a wharf on which they could stand with dry feet while fishing; ran off from his articles of apprenticeship and secured secret passage on a sloop bound for New York under the pretense that he had got a girl with child and would be compelled by her friends to marry her if he remained in Boston; and was in many ways, as he himself said, "too saucy and provoking." Such spirited misdemeanors were not actions to be imitated, and it was the list of Franklin's achievements rather than such details of his boyhood that children were introduced to. The Franklin most often quoted in their readers was Poor Richard. But although his shadow fell upon all nineteenth-century American boys, Franklin was never present to them in the dimension that Washington had been, as young Abraham Lincoln's preference for Weems's *Washington* over Franklin's *Autobiography* indicates. In his beginnings he was so much like the average American boy that his accumulating achievements seemed a reproach to that boy, whereas Washington in the glory of his inimitable actions resisted comparison and discomfited no one. Yet finally it was Franklin with whom Twain began to identify, as the uneasy wavering in his sketch begins to indicate, and similarities are observable in his subsequent writings: Pudd'nhead Wilson's aphorisms in the novel of that name (1895), for example, seem deliberate variations on a theme by Poor Richard.

· · · · ·

Mark Twain read Aldrich's *Story of a Bad Boy* in 1870, the year the book was published, and said then that he found "nothing to admire in it."[17] Whether he changed his mind after he entered into his long friendship with Aldrich is uncertain. What is certain is that the number of incidents in *The Adventures of Tom Sawyer* (1876) that resemble in outline incidents in Aldrich's novel are too many to be coincidental. Twain had found not only his theme in Tom Bailey's "badness," but also a number of the adventures that would illustrate it. In his extensive study of Mark Twain's sources, Walter Blair noted, "Tom Bailey, Aldrich's hero and narrator, anticipates Tom Sawyer: he has a dull time at Sunday school, sneaks out of his bedroom window for night-time adventures, imitates the heroes of books which he has read, camps with other boys on an island where 'we played we were Spanish sailors.'"[18] Although first developed by Aldrich, such incidents were, nevertheless, so typical of boyish adventures that perhaps it is not surprising that Tom Sawyer takes part in them also. But others, such as the extended episode of Tom Sawyer's lovesickness, which Blair goes on to discuss, come too close to Tom Bailey's experience—even to the use of the word "blighted"—to be called typical. In Aldrich's novel, moreover, the drowning that actually did occur while the boys were on their island adventure seems to have suggested to Twain the effects that could be derived from the presumed drowning of Tom Sawyer and his island companions.

To note Twain's indebtedness to Aldrich is not, however, to imply that *The Adventures of Tom Sawyer* is other than the superior narrative that established the bad boy as the model American boy. Writing in *The New Yorker* (April 1960), the critic Dwight MacDonald put it this way: Tom Sawyer "is the All-American boy. He tries to avoid washing, he resists medicine, he plays hooky, he teases the cat, he patronizes the old (ole) swimming hole, he squirms in church, he wriggles in school, he is ritualistically absurd in love, he is fertile in mischief." In actual fact there is no old (ole) swimming hole in *Tom Sawyer*—the Mississippi River is far from that—but we take the point: so normative has the portrait Twain paints become that to recognize it is, for the reader, to bring complementary details to augment it, or, as did Alfred Kazin, to extrapolate from it and see in such boys "future leaders of American enterprise."[19]

A central feature of Twain's book, without parallel in Aldrich's book or others that followed in that vein, is the curious fact that Tom Sawyer is of no specific age. As Marcia Jacobson writes in her shrewd examination of boy books (that is, books for adults that children can read), "No time scheme really fits the book. Tom is young enough to lose a front tooth and old enough to have a crush on a schoolmate. He is in any and all ages of boyhood."[20] This melding of specific ages into a general age that can be called boyhood applies to Tom's mental outlook as well as to matters of fact. He is, for example, horror-stricken at the murder he witnesses and maturely accepts the responsibility of testifying in court against the murderer, yet later in the narrative goes on to organize his companions into a gang of robbers who will kidnap and, if need be, kill. To be sure this is mere make-believe, as Tom well knows, but one can reasonably expect that someone who has witnessed an actual murder as Tom had is too mature for such child's play. Faced with the elasticity of Tom's age, the illustrator of the first edition of *Tom Sawyer* did not construct a single image recognizable as Tom in whatever scene he appeared, but, rather, served up a variety of independent portraits, each suited to a particular incident. At the very outset, for example, he pictured a little scamp of about ten or eleven scaling a fence to escape Aunt Polly, who stands peering after him, and on the facing page pictures a rather well-groomed lad of about fifteen seated at a table with his hand in the sugar bowl while his aunt is turned away from him. Aunt Polly, however, is recognizably the same person in both pictures. The confusion that could result from Tom's randomly progressing and regressing in his chronological age and psychological development as episode follows episode never surfaces, however, because whatever his age at the moment, his moral character remains constant.

Tom Sawyer is an original. Aldrich's Tom Bailey has all the strengths that autobiography can lend him, but, by the same token, has the particularity that makes him *a* bad boy rather than *the* bad boy of American legend. Tom Sawyer, on the other hand, is created out of the materials of boyhood, not the experiences of one boy. He was the first to embody the qualities that after him were trumpeted as the attributes of the typical American boy. Aunt Polly sketches these out: "He warn't *bad* so to say,—only mischievous. Only jest giddy and harum-scarum. . . . *He* warn't any more responsible than a colt. He never meant any harm, and he was the best-hearted boy that ever was." Her friend, Serena Harper, concurs: "It was just so with my Joe—always full of devilment, and up to every mischief, but he was just as unselfish and kind as he could be."

It is in Tom Sawyer's story that his predecessor, the good boy, is definitively evicted from his office as exemplar. Tom "was not the Model Boy of the village. He knew the model boy very well though—and loathed him." Standing in for the dethroned good boy is the annoyingly dutiful Sid, who had "no adventurous troublesome ways." Sid's is not the entrepreneurial spirit that will be rewarded in the industrial America of their adult years. He is closer to the ideal Rollo's father set forth when he told Rollo that he himself had to work "and all people have to do it, and you must learn to do it, or you would grow up indolent and useless." But no longer is this necessarily so. Tom found another way to get the fence whitewashed. When Judge Thatcher heard of the "mighty lie" Tom told to save Becky from a whipping, he said, "with a fine outburst, that it was a noble, a generous, a magnanimous

Tom Sawyer exhibits his "bad boy" credentials.

lie—a lie that was worthy to hold up its head and march down through history breast to breast with George Washington's lauded Truth about the hatchet." Model boyhood had undergone a seismic shift.

Twain's portrait of Tom's hometown, St. Petersburg, is a rich and surprisingly affectionate reconstruction of a provincial Mississippi River village in the lassitude of its prewar isolation. Beyond Aldrich's picture of the Rivermouth of Tom Bailey's boyhood, Twain's is the portrait of a culture as well as of a place. The provincial simplicities bordering upon viciousness that he would elsewhere lash with sarcasm are here forgivingly reassembled in all their risible features, as if, like Tom in his boyhood, the village also was basking in a period of superstitious certainties before the advent of the Civil War would compel it to face up to the responsibilities of adulthood.

Even as he mildly satirizes his townspeople, Twain also savors them. The reader well knows the price that history is going to exact from such sleepy Southern towns, and there is no need for a fictional punishment to be exacted before the war arrives. Everybody in the village believed that Muff Potter had murdered the doctor, and believing so after the fact then believed that before the fact they had already predicted that he would prove a villain. When Tom's testimony proves Muff's innocence, Twain notes that "As usual the fickle, unreasoning world took Muff Potter to its bosom and fondled him as lavishly as it had abused him before. That sort of conduct is to the world's credit; therefore it is not well to find fault with it." The world seen as forgivably fickle and unreasoning is a world in which the imagination, Tom's and Twain's, may play freely. More certain of its truths, the world of the model good boy had previously left scant room for the imagination.

· · · · ·

In the initial planning, Mark Twain appears to have intended to treat Tom's boyhood and youth as the first part of a work that would then carry him forward into the struggles of manhood and end when he returned to St. Petersburg in his late thirties to "meet grown babies & toothless old drivelers who were the grandees of his boyhood." Although he stopped well short of this, he did not, then at least, abandon the idea, but in a letter to Howells said that "by and by I shall take a boy of twelve and run him on through life (in the first person) but not Tom Sawyer—he would not be a good character for it."[21] In the Conclusion to *Tom Sawyer* he explained, "So endeth this chronicle. It being strictly a history of a *boy*, it must stop here; the story could not go much further without becoming the history of a *man*. When one writes a novel about grown people, he knows exactly where to stop—that is, with a marriage; but when he writes of juveniles, he must stop where he best can."

There is, however, ground to suspect that another reason for stopping where he did was that he was uneasy with what he suspected a boy like Tom would be as an adult, and so it was better to leave him where he was, with his newfound wealth, his chivalrous conduct toward Becky, and Judge Thatcher's plan to see that he was appointed to West Point and then sent to law school in order that he might be ready for either career or both. At the book's end, Tom is no longer an outsider. He has been embraced by adult society, and once inside it, the exercise of his daring and ambition could very well lead to less adorable enterprises. E. L. Doctorow brilliantly suggests that "it may even have occurred to Clemens that by some perverse act of literary transmutation he had not anticipated, Tom had replaced Sid as the detestable Model Boy."[22] After all, in 1907, Twain, disgusted with Theodore Roosevelt's imperial adventures, called him "the Tom Sawyer of the political world of the twentieth century."[23]

In the Preface to *Tom Sawyer*, Twain had said, "Although

DESPAIR.

Labeled "Despair," Tom and Becky trapped in the cave

my book is intended for the entertainment of boys and girls, I hope it will not be shunned by men and women on that account, for part of my plan has been to try to pleasantly remind adults of what they once were themselves, and how they felt and thought and talked, and what queer enterprises they sometimes engaged in." But in the year the book was published he also wrote to a childhood friend, Will Bowen, who had, he said, for twenty years stood "dead still in the midst of the dreaminess, the melancholy, the romance, the hysterics of sweet and sappy sixteen. Man, do you know that this is simply mental and moral masturbation? It belongs eminently to the period usually devoted to *physical* masturbation, and should be left there and outgrown."[24] It was one thing to look back and fondly smile at what one once had been, another to fail to emerge from that haze into a consciousness of the world before one.

The letter is as close an indication as we shall receive of Twain's sense of the sexuality of Tom Sawyer and, in an age before Freud and the recognition of childhood sexuality, of the need to bring a boy's story to a close before his sexuality manifested itself. In planning Tom's future, Judge Thatcher was, in effect, relinquishing Becky to him.[25] The boy and girl had in innocence rehearsed the roles of man and wife, and although Twain had said that marriage (and hence the tacit commencement of sexual relations) was an exact stopping point for novels about grown-ups, it was, in a sense, also the stopping point for *Tom Sawyer*. Becky and Tom had spent days together in the dark of the cave before they emerged to receive the Judge's blessing. It was time to draw the curtain.

The arrival of *Huckleberry Finn* eight years after *Tom Sawyer* is powerful evidence that, as Doctorow suggests, Twain sensed that Tom had replaced Sid as the detestable Model Boy. In Huck he would create the true outsider who would flee rather than conform to the ways of his society, who would never, that is, be other than the all-American boy's antithesis.

≡ CITY LIFE ≡

*Ragged Dick, Peck's Bad Boy,
Little Lord Fauntleroy*

The extraordinary rate at which American industry had grown was transforming the social as well as the economic landscape. In 1899, the economist David A. Wells observed that for the generation whose memory went back only to 1860, an account of the economic and industrial experiences of the preceding generation would seem very much like ancient history. There had been 140,000 manufacturing establishments in the United States in 1859, ten years later there were 252,000, and by that year almost a million people lived in the city of New York.[1]

Social reformer Charles Loring Brace, who in his many writings documented the condition of New York's poor, reported in 1872 that thousands upon thousands in that city had no homes, other thousands were connected to crime, while still others worked hard only to see all about them "gilded rewards" that were enjoyed by the rich but that they were not permitted to touch. "Let but Law lift its hand from them for a season," Brace warned, "or let the civilizing influences of American life fail to reach them, and, if the opportunity offered, we should see an explosion from the class which might leave this city in ashes and blood."[2]

For the first twenty years after its founding in 1852, Brace served as secretary of the Children's Aid Society, which had been established by a committee of prominent citizens to improve the lives of the destitute children of the city. An ordained minister, he believed that "Christianity is the highest education of character. Give the poor that, and only seldom would alms or punishment be necessary."[3] But his belief that religious instruction was central to his task did not lessen his efforts to improve the material condition of the children of the poor. Under his supervision, industrial schools and reading rooms were founded, and lodging houses were established to shelter hundreds upon hundreds of homeless children—most in flight from broken families—and bring them within reach of civilizing influences. Brace himself resided in the best known of these residences, the Newsboys Lodging House, which opened in 1854. To it in 1866 came Horatio Alger, Jr., in search of material for his juvenile novels, and there he remained as resident and volunteer assistant for most of the next thirty years, while over the same period he continued to churn out books (more than seventy titles) on the single theme of a poor boy's successful struggle to emerge from poverty. Identical in character, his heroes were commonly differentiated by their initial occupations rather than any distinctive trait of personality—Dick the bootblack, Mark the match boy, and Ben the luggage boy were essentially the same boy—while in his occasional forays into biography, he presented Daniel Webster, the "farm boy," Abraham Lincoln, the "backwoods boy," and James Garfield, the "canal boy." Repetitive plot lines and increasingly neglectful prose reflected the speed at which Alger managed all this. Yet for all the vast difference between his formulaic success stories—pep talks for American boys—and Brace's comprehensive studies of the urban poor—blueprints for social action—it was Alger who brought to the printed page an implicit, albeit not quite intended, recognition that the conditions of big city life were revising the nation's moral as well as its social values. Big city conditions were not an amplified version of everyday conditions in a smaller city. Rather, the massive change in the number of people grouped together day in and day out redefined acceptable moral as well as social conduct. Quantitative change, that is, meant qualitative change.

When Benjamin Franklin, the prototypical poor boy destined for success, first arrived in Philadelphia from Boston and took his fabled stroll from the Delaware River wharf into the city, shirts and stockings stuffed into his pockets, with a puffy roll under each arm while he munched a third, his wealth amounted to the change he had received for the Dutch dollar with which he had purchased the rolls. The city he then entered had a population of ten thousand, which would steadily increase until in the year American independence was declared there, Philadelphia with its forty thousand inhabitants was second in size only to London among British cities. A town of that size was unlike any previously known American community, and in the manual of advice that the successful Franklin provided for young men in his *Autobiography* he described the kind of conduct required for success in the unprecedented circumstances of city life. Virtue alone might signify in a small community whose residents were known to each other from infancy, but in the city of strangers even the virtues one truly possessed were of limited value if one were not seen to possess them. He explained that at the commencement of his business career he was not only industrious but took care that others saw his industriousness, and so he publicly performed as well as privately practiced his virtues: "I took care not only to be in *Reality* industrious and frugal, but to avoid all *Appearances* to the contrary," he wrote. "To show that I was not above my business I sometimes brought home the paper I purchased at the stores through the streets on a wheelbarrow."[4] Those who saw him already knew his name; now they learned what he was made of.

But such displays were not of much avail in the city of a million, where rich, poor, and middling classified the nameless others they daily passed on the streets in terms of appearance rather than performance. In Alger's tales, the poor boy, however industrious and frugal, will continue to be perceived as a member of the destitute class so long as he appears to be one. While for Alger it is, to be sure, a truism that to succeed a poor boy must be an honest, hardworking boy, that in itself will not start a rise in social standing; passersby will continue to classify him as, in Brace's term, a member of the "dangerous" classes. Diligence in performing his tasks might mark him as a superior bootblack, but he still remained only a bootblack. To move upward he had to already appear to be what in reality he had not yet become; to seem, that is, to be a member, however lowly, of the class of those who earned their income behind the doors of offices and shops rather than on the streets. For Alger (as a generation later it would be for Theodore Dreiser in his great novels of individuals astray in metropolitan America), appearing in respectable dress was a prerequisite for, rather than the result of, a change of fortune. Virtue is a moral quality, not in itself manifest to the eye of the casual observer, but respectability is a social quality apparent to the eye, and success depends upon it. To be sure, those who have money dress more attractively than those who do not, but in their careers Alger's poor boys reverse that causal relationship. It does them little good to have earned money if they fail to invest it in a presentable suit of clothing, in, that is, respectability, and they typically emerge from the anonymity of their class by expending their hard-earned savings on their appearance before attending to other wants. To advance they must not seem as poor as they actually are.

Ragged Dick is fortunate enough to attract the attention of a well-to-do youth, who, wishing him well, provides him with a suit of presentable, if cast-off, clothing. This enables Dick, in turn, to empty his small savings account in order to outfit his bootblack chum, Fosdick, so that Fosdick can apply for a position as shop assistant.

"Though I hope my readers will not suspect him of being a dude," Alger says of another of his protagonists, Luke Larkin, "he certainly did enjoy the consciousness of being well dressed," and this is obviously a factor in the benevolent Mr. Armstrong reflecting, "A thoroughly good boy, and a smart boy too! I must see if I can give him a chance to rise." Being smart in the commercial world also means being smartly dressed. When Luke is commissioned to travel on business, he is told, "Bring a supply of underclothing."

In the novel in which he is the protagonist, Jed, who is "poorly dressed" at first, acquires a "brown suit, with clean linen," whereupon "his personal appearance would do credit to any family however exclusive. Yet he had been brought up in a Scranton poorhouse, and associated with paupers all his life." In a hint of Gatsby, yet thirty years off, Jed is employed on wealthy Schuyler Roper's yacht, where he is again sent off to "procure clothing, undergarments, et cetera."

Those from their own class who knew and liked Dick, Luke, Jed, and others before they were well dressed scarcely recognize them in their changed attire. They knew the boys were good, but now they see that they are also respectable, which is to say they now appear worthy of the esteem of those beyond their little circle. In the new metropolis, virtue unclad will not translate into respectability. Moreover, once attained, their respectability separates Dick and the others from both their former acquaintances and their former selves.[5] Moving up means moving out.

Early in *Ragged Dick*, Alger tells us, "There were not a few young clerks who employed Dick from time to time in his professional capacity, who scarcely earned as much as he, greatly as their style and dress exceeded his." This is not, however, a homily in favor of the thrift Dick has practiced. Rather, it is an introduction to the need to spend money on clothes. In a way that matters more than present income, those clerks are better off than Dick because they are better situated to rise in the city of appearances. Of Dick's friend Fosdick, in search of a position that will take him off the streets and into a shop, Alger writes, "When he obtained a place he could not expect to receive as much as he was now making from blacking boots—probably not more than three dollars [which thirty shoe shines could earn him] while his expenses without clothing would amount to four dollars." Yet there is no question but that Fosdick is moving in the right direction.

In Alger's books, the bad boy who is contrasted with the good boy is not the bully from the poor boy's class who occasionally pesters him and is always soundly thumped, but the boy from more comfortable economic circumstances who sneers at ragged clothing, scorns mean labor, and, with persistent wrongheadedness, insists in tale after tale that because he is better dressed and has never dirtied his hands with work, he is better qualified for the job in office or shop that will, however, ultimately be awarded not to him but to the poor boy, once that poor boy is respectably clothed. But not until then.

Although they appeared in books written after the Civil War, Aldrich's Tom Bailey and Twain's Tom Sawyer enjoyed their youth in the antebellum period. But growing up in the years after the war, Alger's stereotyped heroes were so exclusively concerned with emerging from their distressed condition that they lacked the leisure to engage in the kind of mischief that in an earlier period had endeared "bad" boys to readers; indeed, in their straitened circumstances such rascality would endanger their efforts to seem respectable. The "rags to riches" fable that was later to be attached to the Alger boy had no factual base in the actual plots of his novels, but was a product of the 1920s adoration of wealthy men who had begun their careers in modest or worse circumstances.[6] The rise that Ragged Dick and his like did manage to achieve was far short of "riches," but no less important: they had moved off the street into shops and offices and now received a regular wage. To seek out further Alger novels after having read one of them is to take pleasure in the constantly reiterated parable of a poor boy overcoming the obstacles to commercial success presented by cruel guardians, mean rich boys, and big city confidence tricksters. What that boy can count upon in his assorted travails is that the law will always be on his side and not the villain's; that, in effect, American society is benevolent and well worth the struggle to gain admission to it.

Horatio Alger was the most prolific of the first group of novelists who portrayed life in big city America. He depicted the metropolis as the site of opportunity, while Charles Loring Brace, who knew the sociological details of that life far better than Alger, was architect of the Children's Aid Society's "emigration" policy, which saw the city as the site of vice and placed poor children with families in the country. The policy rested on the principle that the best of all asylums for the child was the farmer's home, where, Brace said, a process of "moral disinfection" could take place. But whatever might be said for the obvious benefits of fresh air, fresh food, and productive labor that would come to the boy placed with a caring farm family, his move from city to farm was also a move upstream against the current of history. Although the nation's rural population increased absolutely in the decades following the Civil War, the proportion of the total population actually living on farms steadily declined.[7] Farm boys entered the city in increasing numbers to seek better-remunerated and more varied employments than the farm (which itself was being industrialized) had to offer. If many were attracted by the city's night life, they were also drawn to the city's libraries, evening schools, and cultural events. Yet even as commerce throve and cities swelled, Brace's God remained in the country. Alger saw him present on city streets.[8]

· · · · ·

In *Ragged Dick, or Street Life in New York with Boot Blacks* (1868), "our hero," as Alger calls Dick, is talking with Johnny, a fellow bootblack, when Johnny abruptly dodges into an entryway to hide behind the door. When Dick asks him the reason for this, Johnny, "his voice betraying anxiety," asks whether he has gone. "Who?" asks Dick. "The man in the brown coat," says Johnny, saying he is scared because the man in the brown coat is the one who once got him the place in the country from which he ran away. He is afraid that if the man sees him he will send him back to the country. Johnny admits that he had a good bed and plenty to eat on the farm, but when Dick asks why he didn't stay, he answers, "I felt lonely."

Alger then steps in to say:

> Johnny could not exactly explain his feelings, but it is often the case that the young vagabond of the streets, though his food is uncertain, and his bed may be an old wagon or barrel that he is lucky enough to find unoccupied when night sets in, gets so attached to his precarious but independent mode of life, that he feels discontented in any other. He is accustomed to the noise and bustle and ever-varied life of the streets, and in the quiet scenes of the country misses the excitement in the midst of which he has always dwelt.

In *Tom Sawyer*, Huck Finn had preferred his nights in a barrel to the security of comfortable lodgings in Widow Douglas's house, and in *Huckleberry Finn*, published the year before *Ragged Dick*, he carried his flight from civilization further. But although the independence Huck seeks is different in kind from Johnny's, and despite the manifest difference in literary quality that may seem to undermine comparison between the two novels, there is another similarity that is of greater significance than nights spent in a barrel. Huck ultimately flees to Indian Territory in order to preserve his independence; in order to regain his, Johnny flees back to the crowded streets of New York, where violence always threatens, stealth is always required, and nomadism is a condition of everyday life. As Brace recognized, this too was an Indian Territory. "There seemed to be a very considerable class of lads in New York," he wrote, "who bore to the busy, wealthy world about them something of the same relation which Indians bear to the civilized Western settlers,"[9] their principles no better than savages'. In so saying, he also endorsed the widely held psychological belief that in the stages of his development a growing boy recapitulates the history of society from savagery to civilization.[10]

The theory was also reflected, albeit in less determining form, in both Aldrich's Tom Bailey and Twain's Tom Sawyer. When a group of Wyandotte Indians pass through town on their way to an involuntary resettlement, the boys in Aldrich's novel envy what they believe to be the Indians' carefree way of life, wishing they could be like them, and on their island adventure Tom, Huck, and Joe Harper strip naked and play Indian for a day. That Tom's nemesis, Injun Joe, is an actual Indian suggests that in testifying against him Tom is outgrowing the primitive stage of his life.[11]

Charles Dudley Warner, Twain's Hartford neighbor and friend who had collaborated in the writing of *The Gilded Age* (1875), Twain's first novel, said in the account of his own boyhood, "Every boy who is good for anything is a natural savage. . . . You want to catch your boy young, and study him before he has either virtues or vices, in order to understand the primitive man."[12]

As the nineteenth century advanced, however, others saw more viciousness than charm in the savagery of boyhood. In the memoir of his early years, generalized to represent the contents of a typical American boyhood, William Dean Howells wrote:

The Young People may have heard it said that a savage is a grown-up child but it seems to me even more true that a child is a savage. Like the savage he dwells on an earth round which the whole solar system revolves, and he is himself the centre of all life on the earth. It has no meaning but as it relates to him; it is for his pleasure, and his use; it is for his pain and his abuse.[13]

As he gets more deeply into the narrative, detailing the behavior of the boys he knew and the boy he was, Howells becomes even more biting in his critique: "In their ideals and ambitions they were foolish and in most of their intentions they were mischievous." Unlike "mischievous" in the sense idealized by Tom Sawyer's behavior, the term now carries the meaning of barbarous. Howells continues, startlingly in view of the affectionate view of human nature his novels exuded: "They have no conception of generosity. . . . They seldom laugh except at the pain or shame of some one. . . . They lived in a state of outlawry, in the midst of invisible terrors, and they knew no rule but that of might."[14]

Raised in Ohio towns before the Civil War, Howells made his professional life in the East. He was living in New York when he wrote the recollections of his boyhood, and the acerbity of his generalizations on boyhood outlawry attaches uncomfortably to the pleasant episodes that make up the substance of his book. It is as if his dismay at what the America he once knew had become after its euphoric emergence from the war had stained the memories of his earlier life. He was not alone in his dismay. In 1871, the once exuberant Walt Whitman characterized American society as "cankered, crude, superstitious, and rotten." "It was," he wrote, "as if we were endowed with a vast and thoroughly appointed body, and then left with little or no soul."[15]

· · · · ·

In *The Story of a Bad Boy* (1870) Aldrich had reversed the good boy/bad boy distinction, saying that he "wished simply to draw a line at the start between his hero—a natural, actual boy—and that unwholesome and altogether improbable little prig, which had hitherto been held up as an example to the young." The reversed distinction achieved iconic status in the persons of Tom Sawyer and Sid, but as the century advanced, the good/bad distinction underwent a radical polarization. The mischievous boy who continued to be presented as the typical and likeable American boy turned so worldly-wise that his well-behaved opposite, who had meanwhile become increasingly guileless, gained in attractiveness. *Peck's Bad Boy and His Pa* (1883), by George Wilbur Peck, a best seller in its day (together with its supplements, it went on to sell over a million copies), exemplified the new, worldly bad boy. At the opposite pole was Frances Hodgson Burnett's *Little Lord Fauntleroy* (1886), an immense favorite as a novel, then as a play that remained in the repertory of touring companies for decades before reappearing in the twentieth century as a popular film. So popular was the little lord that he served as a fashion plate as well as a model of conduct, and to the distress of at least one generation of American boys, inspired their mothers to dress them in black velvet. In the opening series of sketches, Peck's popular boy, Hennery, concentrated exclusively on inflicting pain on cats, dogs, and humans, with his father serving as the principal target of torment, while in his story the little lord was tirelessly affectionate toward the maid, the grocer, and the boys on his New York street before crossing the Atlantic to be equally nice to all members of the English aristocracy, their servants, their horses, and their dogs. Both Hennery and Fauntleroy had a large following, and although, given their immense popularity, there must have been some overlap in the membership of their respective audiences, they occupied sharply opposed social and political positions.

George Wilbur Peck (1840–1916) is notable in the history of American politics for being one of the first candidates to have been elected to prominent offices as a result of a celebrity earned outside of politics or military service. He was a journalist and within that profession an entertainer. Born in New York state, Peck moved to Wisconsin at an early age and there began a working life that followed a familiar American pattern: from printer, to country editor, to writer of newspaper sketches and authorship of the books into which they were gathered. During the Civil War, he served in the Fourth Wisconsin, editing the regimental newspaper; then reentering civilian life in the late 1860s, he took over the Ripon *Representative* and converted it from a Republican to a fiercely partisan Democratic newspaper. He first attracted national attention in 1869 with a series of letters he published in another partisan newspaper, the New York *Democrat*. In them, Terence McGrant, a fictional cousin of the president, talked of the scandals in the Grant administration and complained that the president thought more of "nagers and dogs" than he did of his relatives.

In 1874, Peck founded the *Sun* in La Crosse, soon renaming it *Peck's Sun*, and four years later moved it to Milwaukee, scene of the popular "bad boy" sketches that he wrote for it. *Peck's Sun* was essentially a humorous periodical consisting in the main of satirical sketches that were soon after gathered together and published as books: *Peck's Fun*, the first collection, appeared in 1879 and was followed by other compilations in 1882, 1883, and 1884. All found some favor with the reading public, but *Peck's Bad Boy and His Pa* went beyond provincial acclaim to make its author famous nationally. Published by a Chicago firm in 1883, the thirty-six sketches in *Peck's Bad Boy and His Pa* enjoyed so large an immediate success that within the same year a second series consisting of twenty-seven sketches was published. Subsequent editions, frequently reprinted, contained both series. With the push given by his literary fame, Peck entered politics and in 1890 was elected mayor of Milwaukee in a landslide victory, then in the following year left that office after having been elected governor of Wisconsin in another landslide victory. He was reelected to a second term as governor, but thereafter failed to be reelected, although he sought the office again on several occasions.

Each of the bad boy Hennery's escapades in *Peck's Bad Boy and His Pa* is narrated in the first person by Hennery himself. In the first four sketches Peck varied the setting of each of Hennery's accounts of the most recent practical joke he had played upon his father, then in the fifth hit upon the scenario in which Hennery was to detail each of the remaining fifty-nine pranks that he played upon Pa, almost all of them blithely sadistic. His violent antics looked both back to the vicious yet brilliantly executed sketches of the Southwestern humorist G. W. Harris, who wrote under the name Sut Lovingood in the 1860s, and forward to the dismembering capers of twentieth-century animated cartoon figures, in which cats, coyotes, and other comically threatening creatures are singed, flattened, or exploded, only to be reassembled and available for future dismemberment in succeeding installments. Since Pa, for all his abundant faults, is a father who does, from time to time, attempt to reach out to his son, the unfailing tortures he undergoes at his son's hands would soon tire (if not appal) did not Hennery's attacks upon his pretensions represent a larger assault upon society's unquestioned proprieties.

A number of Hennery's tricks are physical. Knowing his father likes macaroni, for example, he cuts a rubber hose into macaroni shapes and mixes them in Pa's dish; pours cod liver oil instead of syrup on Pa's pancakes; hands Pa caustic instead of ointment to spread on his sores; agitates a hornet's nest when Pa is napping under it; trains a dog to attach his teeth to the seat of Pa's pants; arranges for a terrified cat to drop down upon Pa's head; hands Pa a gun that backfires; and, needless to say, on July 4th sees to it that the fireworks blow up all around and upon Pa.

In another group of inflictions the aim is to hurt Pa psychologically rather than physically; that is, to humiliate him in his social aspirations. In response to Pa's attempts to acquire the social status that accompanies admission into church membership in a middle-American Protestant community, Hennery assiduously sees to it that Pa's claims to sobriety and sincerity are subverted by, for example, planting playing cards in the handkerchief Pa pulls from his pocket in church, and, for good measure, soaking that handkerchief in rum. Pa also aims at the social advantage that comes from being a veteran of the Grand Army of the Republic, but, as

In church, Pa unwittingly takes out a rum-soaked
handkerchief wrapped around playing cards.

Hennery discovers, his war service was as a sutler and the provision he supplied to the troops was pepper sauce in alcohol labeled as whiskey.

In another series of psychological assaults, Hennery concentrates upon exploiting Pa's appetite for sexual dalliance. He dresses up a friend in girl's clothes, arranging for his mother to come upon Pa hugging the supposed girl; or, in another episode, drapes borrowed female garments around Pa's bedroom for his mother to discover when she returns from an out-of-town visit.

These practical, and almost always cruel, jokes can be seen, finally, to be focused through Pa at the hypocrisy of middle-class life in mid-America. Although they derive their primary power from their Oedipal source—Hennery does his dreadful best to remove his father from the marital scene—his target also expands to the minister and the deacons of the church Pa longs to enter, who are revealed to be hypocrites also; ministers always drink, he learns, when they go to Chicago. In *Peck's Bad Boy and His Pa* the proprieties that govern Midwestern society are under free-swinging assault while, in parallel, the revelation of the actual service Pa performed in the Civil War tacitly confronts the era's tiresome political summoning of the Civil War—the waving of the bloody shirt—as justification for continued Republican possession of the White House. The savage practical jokes could not in themselves have attracted so wide a following were not the exposure of Pa's hypocrisies an unproclaimed assault upon the social practices and political beliefs he attempted to associate himself with, such as the unchallenged esteem associated with church membership or with having worn the Union uniform.

Peck's racial biases are blatant: Hennery, for example, says, "There's an Italian got a bear that performs in the street, and I am going to find where he is showing, and feed the bear a cayenne pepper lozenger, and see him clear out the Polack settlement," and this, apparently, damaged neither the size of his readership nor his political aspirations. For a large number of readers there seems to have been something deeply satisfying about such conventionally unmentionable racial sentiments erupting to the surface under the protection of their occurrence in a comic world where wounds appeared to heal quickly. Peck goes further, attacking sanctimoniousness itself regardless of what it is attached to. Hennery appears to be assisting the streetcar driver by turning the brake to stop the car for a Sister of Charity, only, when the driver's back is turned, to prod the mule with a fishing pole to see if he can flip her off the back step. *Peck's Bad Boy and His Pa* is a seething theater in which widespread if unarticulated discontents with the smug certainties of American life are acted out.

The sketches are both sadistic and racist. Yet they also sound reveille for what historians would later call the "revolt of the village" in describing the writings of those sons of the Middle West who fled their homes in order to free their pens, and with neither sadism nor racism (or just a bit of it) took up themes that Peck had opened, attacking the idols of their native land with force and finesse: Edgar Lee Masters's *Spoon River Anthology* (1915), Sherwood Anderson's *Winesburg, Ohio* (1919), and Sinclair Lewis's *Main Street* (1920) are three prominent examples. *Peck's Bad Boy* is their wrathful proletarian predecessor.

· · · · ·

The most powerful contribution to the thematic force of *Peck's Bad Boy and His Pa*, however, resides not in the pranks themselves, but in the format into which Peck inserted them. Starting with the fifth, each episode opens with Hennery entering the grocery store, and then, most often in response to the grocer's asking why he looks so poorly or why his Pa has been seen in town in so battered a condition, Hennery describes the latest joke he played upon Pa.

When his account ends, he exchanges a further remark or two with the grocer and then departs, and it is in what characteristically happens upon his entrance and his exit that Peck establishes the aura of corruption that permeates the world of Hennery's exploits.

A sketch in which Hennery tells of training a dog to assault Pa begins, for example:

> "If the dogs in our neighborhood hold out I guess I can do something that all the temperance societies in this town have failed to do," says the bad boy to the grocery man, as he cut off a piece of cheese and took a handful of crackers out of a box.
>
> "Well for Heaven's sake, what have you been doing now, you little reprobate?" asked the grocery man, as he went to the desk and charged the boy's father with a pound and four ounces of cheese and two pounds of crackers.

Hennery's story soon follows, and when it finishes the boy, making a comment such as that about his plan for the Italian's trained bear, leaves to execute further mischief.

Each visit to the grocery starts and usually ends with Hennery, uninvited, helping himself to or attempting to purloin some provision, the cost of which the grocer duly amplifies in Pa's account—a stick of cinnamon is set down as half a pound; a cracker dipped into a barrel of syrup is charged as a pound of crackers and a gallon of syrup—while the boy, ever alert to steal what he can, after leaving the grocery frequently contrives to pin a notice on its door, such as "Spoiled Canned Ham And Tongue Good Enough For Church Picnics" or "Yellow Sand Wanted For Maple Sugar." The sweet potatoes in the grocery are not as large as advertised, the produce delivered is not the produce that is displayed, the grocer throws a rotten potato into a basket of good ones that are going to the orphan asylum.[16] The constant byplay of dishonesty between

boy and grocer, its (not unfunny) unscrupulousness under-
lined by the nonchalance with which it takes place, sets the
values of the world in which Hennery's view of life is established. The omnipresence of corruption invades Hennery's
similes as well. Speaking of the tomcat he employed to attack
Pa, he tells the grocer, "It isn't afraid of anything, and can whip
a Newfoundland dog quicker than you can put sand in a barrel of sugar." When the parrot he has taught to speak rudely
disrupts the meeting of the church committee taking place in
Ma's parlor—"What are you giving us?" the parrot behind the
window curtain replies after the minister's prayer—"I was
sitting on a piano stool," Hennery tells the grocer, "as pious as
a Sunday School superintendent the Sunday before he skips
out with the bank's funds."

In his introductory remarks to the complete edition of
Peck's Bad Boy and His Pa, Peck wrote, "The 'Bad Boy' is not a
myth," but is located "in every city, village, and country hamlet throughout the land." He will be naughty, "but he shuffles
through life until the time comes for him to make his mark
in the world, and then he buckles on the harness and goes
to the front and he becomes successful." A sharp reproof to
the determined honesty of Ragged Dick and associates, but,
indeed, if American society was as vitiated as Hennery and
the grocer illustrate it to have been, then Hennery was on
his way to becoming a successful businessman, industrial-
ist, or politician rather than a penitentiary inmate. An article
in *Leslie's Weekly* (1898) praising Admiral Dewey, who had
seized the Philippines, noted that as a boy he was a "harum-
scarum lad" who was not "over particular as to who owned
the trees from which he picked apples."[17]

Roscoe Conkling, United States senator from New York
from 1867 to his death in 1888, known for his power as Republican Party organizer and spoils distributor rather than for
any public policy he advocated, said that "When Dr. Johnson
defined patriotism as the last refuge of a scoundrel, he was

unconscious of the then undeveloped capabilities and use of the word *reform*." That was the America of Peck's bad boy.

· · · · ·

I n 1936, David O. Selznick had a plaque put up on the wall at 1215 I Street in Washington, D.C. It reads, "ON THIS SITE FIFTY YEARS AGO THE DEATHLESS CLASSIC LITTLE LORD FAUNTLEROY WAS WRITTEN." There may be some characteristic Hollywood hyperbole in this, but not much. If not a "classic," *Little Lord Fauntleroy* (1886) is certainly an extraordinarily accomplished piece of children's literature, which like all superior works in that category enjoys an adult audience equal in size to, perhaps greater than, the juvenile. The novel's fairy-tale premise evolves seamlessly into an engaging story, marred only by the denouement's dependence upon a preposterous coincidence. But by then it is too late for the captured reader, intent upon arriving at the removal of the last obstacle to Cedric's patrimony, to do other than accept coincidence for the sake of a happy ending.

Born in Manchester, England, Frances Hodgson Burnett (1849–1924), the little lord's creator, emigrated to the United States in 1865 when her widowed mother, Eliza Hodgson, responded to the invitation of her brother, who had a dry goods store in Knoxville, and moved to that city with her children. A writer of stories from her earliest years, Frances Hodgson received her first acceptance from the prestigious *Godey's Ladies Book* and continued to write steadily in support of her mother and her siblings. After her marriage in 1873 to an ophthalmologist, Swan Moses Burnett, her writing provided the chief financial support for their family, which came to include two sons, Lionel (born in 1874, died of tuberculosis in 1890) and Vivian (born in 1876), while Dr. Burnett concentrated more upon research than upon developing a remunerative practice. In 1877, in pursuit of the doctor's professional interests, the family moved from Knoxville to Washington, D.C., and with her literary fame expanding, Burnett (the surname she used for the remainder of her career) began to travel away from home for extended periods, making prolonged stays in New York and London, where she numbered Israel Zangwill and Henry James among her friends. Her absences from home transgressed what the age considered to be her marital duties, but despite the tattling about her conduct she maintained unbroken a close and loving relationship with her sons both in that period and after her divorce from the doctor in 1896.

Burnett's first novel, *That Lass O'Lowrie* (1877), was set in a Lancashire mining community that she depicted with an exacting attention to realistic detail, including dialogue in the local dialect. But she departed from such precisely localized material in the many stories and more than twenty adult novels that followed, deliberately pointing her work toward commercial success and candidly labeling herself "a pen-driving machine." *Little Lord Fauntleroy* was the first children's story she wrote, and it remained the most widely known of them for more than a century, although *The Secret Garden* (1911), undeniably its literary superior, now appears to have overtaken *Fauntleroy* in popularity. *The Secret Garden*, pace Mr. Selznick, is truly a children's classic.

• • • • •

Recalling the inception of *Little Lord Fauntleroy*, Burnett said that her young son Vivian had asked her, "When a person is a duke, what makes him one?" He evidently thought "dukedom was a species of reward for sweetness of character and brilliant intellectual capacity." And so she began to imagine a brilliant little republican in contact with a real duke, and thinking she would write a story, figured that the way boy and duke would come into contact was through the boy being the child of the duke's youngest son, who had become alienated from him when he married an American woman who possessed neither wealth nor social prominence.[18] The novel began to run in the children's magazine *St. Nicholas* in November 1885, and in the following year the book was published in a first edition of ten thousand, but before those copies reached the stores reprinting had begun.

Little Cedric Errol lives in New York with his mother, the widow of Captain Cedric Errol. He has only a vague memory of his father, who he knows was an Englishman, but responsive to his mother's sensitivity on the matter he does not wish to bring further tears to her eyes by speaking of him. He does, however, always address his mother as "Dearest," because he remembers that was what his father always called her. Seven-year-old Cedric's days are spent in playing with the boys in his neighborhood. One of his friends is Dick, a shoe shine boy older than he. They first met when Cedric was yet a baby. When Cedric's ball had slipped from his fingers and rolled into traffic, Dick had dashed under the wheels of a horse-drawn carriage to retrieve it.

Cedric also has adult friends. Mary, the maid of all work in his house, holds long conversations with him on such momentous subjects as the recent presidential election. This would have been that of 1884, when Grover Cleveland became the first Democrat since the Civil War to have been elected, because Cedric, who declares himself to be a " 'publican," tells Mary, who is Irish and a "dimmycrat," that "the country will go to ruin." But his special friend is Mr. Hobbs the grocer, with whom he holds equally ingenuous discussions on the glories of democratic and the vices of aristocratic society.

One day Mr. Havisham, an English solicitor, comes to call on Cedric's mother. He had been sent by the Earl of Dorincourt with the news that the first and second of the Earl's three sons had both died childless, and since, unbeknownst to Cedric, his father was the Earl's third son, he, Cedric, was now heir to the earldom and was being summoned to Dorin-court to enter upon preparation for the great responsibilities he would eventually assume. So accompanied by his mother Cedric is taken to live with his grandfather, and in the course of his first year in England, with which the greater part of the novel is concerned, he wins over the ill-humored, overbear-ing Earl by his unstinting goodwill and artless ignorance of the fact that all who know the Earl, from fellow aristocrats, to tenants, to servants, dislike and fear the intolerant old man. To the trusting Cedric, however, his grandfather appears to be as benevolent as he is mighty, even as the reader recognizes that his apparent benevolence is only an indulgence of Ced-ric's childish wish to help others. As the grandfather's love for his grandson takes hold, however, he begins to derive plea-sure himself from the good deeds that please Cedric, and as their relationship grows, the little republican in training to be an aristocrat unconsciously trains the elderly autocrat to be what he in his innocence always believed him to be, a paternal benefactor to all below him. Burnett thus adroitly manages to let her public have it both ways in a Cinderella story that feeds the undying American fascination with the furnishings and protocols of aristocratic high life while at the same time asserting the natural superiority of republican principles.

Throughout her narrative, Burnett makes it clear that she is a storyteller through whose voice the story is reaching the reader. She does not remove the story from everyday life with so apparent a device as "once upon a time," but, never-theless, achieves a similar distancing, constantly making her presence felt with such locutions as "There was never a more amazed boy than Cedric" (rather than "Cedric was amazed") or saying toward the close, "And that would be the end of my story except..."

• • • • •

L *ittle Lord Fauntleroy* is always implicitly, and also at times explicitly, in conversation with two previous models of American boy life, Alger's upward-bound poor boy and Peck's worldly bad boy. Dick, the bootblack friend of little Cedric, cannot but be Alger's Ragged Dick resurrected: "He had been a street waif nearly all his life," Burnett wrote, "and he always had a private yearning for a respectable kind of existence. Since he had been in business for himself, he had made enough money to enable him to sleep under a roof instead of out in the streets, and he had begun to hope he might reach even a higher place in time." That is pure Alger, albeit better phrased.

The characteristic turning point in the life of an Alger boy occurs when he attracts the attention of a philanthropic bystander by performing one or another unselfish act, such as that of Dick when he dives into the traffic to recover little Cedric's ball. The eventual reward for the Alger protagonist's performance is a position that promises a successful commercial future. Dick, who figures in the coincidence that brings about the denouement of *Little Lord Fauntleroy*, is rewarded by the Earl of Dorincourt with the means to acquire an education, arguably a more helpful push toward a successful career than the more commonplace job Alger usually provided the poor boy. But both are upward-bound.

In 1899, the year of Alger's death, his *Jed, the Poorhouse Boy* was published. The exhaustion that had for some time been yawning over his stories was now all but paralyzing. After a brief exercise of manful energy in standing up to a contemptible poorhouse superintendent and going into the world on his own, Jed drifts along passively, relying upon happenstance to carry him forward. Ragged Dick and his ilk worked hard at the success they sought, even though luck frequently came to their aid, but Jed initiates nothing after he flees the poorhouse. He is the product of whatever happens to him. In one chain of incidents he becomes the victim of a confidence scheme, vows not to be fooled again, and then is similarly victimized time and again while Alger thinks about some way to help him succeed. This finally arrives in the person of the wealthy Schuyler Roper, who takes a fancy to him and appoints him assistant on his yacht, a paid and, one might justly say, a kept companion.

In his first adventure away from the poorhouse, Jed had gone to the theater in a nearby town, invited to attend the performance by an actor whom he met the night before. As chance would have it, the boy actor in the play to be presented by the professional company that night has taken ill. Jed is quickly auditioned, found to be a quick learner, and put into the part, which although not large is crucial to the plot. Since the boy actor remains too ill to perform, Jed tours with the company until the season ends, but then, adrift on the Jersey shore and later in New York, never manages to hold a job until the yachtsman discovers him.

One day in New York the wandering Jed chats with a newsboy and tells him that he had for a brief time been an actor. Were you Little Lord Fauntleroy? the boy asks. No, he wasn't, Jed says. But he did play the telegraph boy in *The Gold King*, a drama in which the wealthy title character is in search of his lost son who had been snatched away some years ago, and, in the last act, finds that the telegraph boy is his long-lost child. With that dramatic transformation in mind, abetted by the newsboy's suggestion, what should Alger do at the close of the novel but reveal that Jed, who was presumably a foundling, had in his infancy been left at the poorhouse door by a woman who had been suborned to do so by Guy, the brother of Sir Charles Fenwick, of Fenwick Hall, Gloucestershire, so that Guy could inherit his brother's title. Sir Charles died believing that his infant son had died many years before him when, in point of fact, Jed is that son. And so at novel's close he is recognized to be Sir Robert Fenwick, of Fenwick Hall, Alger thus concluding his borrowings from Burnett's novel. But if, chronologically, Alger had the last word (Fauntleroy followed Ragged Dick but then Jed followed Fauntleroy), thematically he had capitulated by abandoning pluck and hard work, the Alger boy's reliable formula for success, in favor of the happy circumstance of a fortunate birth.

Peck's Bad Boy also participates in Burnett's conversation with her predecessors. In his New York childhood, Cedric "was fond of the milkman and the baker and the applewoman," but "his greatest friend was the grocery man at the corner." His name was Mr. Hobbs, and Cedric "was on such terms of intimacy with him that he went to see him every day and sat with him quite a long time, discussing the topics of the hour." In view of Hennery's daily visits to the grocer in *Peck's Bad Boy*, it seems certain that Burnett's choice of a grocer for Cedric's daily visits rather than any other merchant or craftsman is a pointed response to Peck, with Cedric's innocence and Mr. Hobbs's naïveté designedly opposed to Hennery's worldliness and the grocer's dishonesty. Even as Hennery keeps a sharp eye out to pilfer what provisions he can during his conversations with the grocer, Cedric sits and eats apples from the box and crackers from the barrel while the hospitable Mr. Hobbs and he hold their discussions on matters of state. The marked contrast to Hennery's larcenous exchanges with the grocer has a political dimension as well, shaped by the cynical realism of Peck's Democratic connections and the certainties of Burnett's Republican affiliations—she was a next-door neighbor of James A. Garfield when he was in Congress and remained a close friend after he entered the White House.[19] (The fact that the maiden name of Burnett's mother-in-law was Peck tantalizes—make of it what one will.)

· · · · ·

Cedric was a "sweet baby." He had "long eyelashes," "gold-colored curly hair," and when he went out with his nurse,

Cedric and Mr. Hobbs discuss the superiority of the American social system.

dragging his wagon along the street, "he wore a short white kilt skirt." As he grew, his was a "graceful childish figure in a black velvet suit, with a lace collar, and with lovelocks waving about the handsome manly face." When in their frequent fond conversations about Cedric after he has departed for England, Dick the bootblack talks to Hobbs the grocer about Cedric, he says that when Cedric was younger "he'd holler: 'Hello Dick,' at me, as friendly as if he was six feet high, when he warn't knee high to a grasshopper, and was dressed in gal's close."

Reginald Birch furnished the illustrations for *Little Lord Fauntleroy* that fixed his image in the minds of most readers. In picturing the lovelocks, the lace collar, and the black velvet suit with trousers that stopped at the knees, giving way to red stockings, perhaps he went a step beyond what Burnett had pictured in words, especially when Cedric is illustrated wearing his characteristic velvet suit even when astride a pony, but Burnett certainly does emphasize the girlishness of Cedric's features both in her descriptions—especially the repeated references to his long golden locks—and in the fond memories of him his friends have. In all of Birch's pictures save one, Cedric is shown in the company of adults or animals rather than children, and so his image can be taken to be that of a boy. In the one exception, however, Cedric is racing down a New York street alongside (but slightly ahead of) a boy who wears a cap and long trousers, and in that setting Cedric in his shorter trousers with his tresses floating behind him would be taken to be a girl if the text did not speak differently.

To note this, however, is neither to suggest that Cedric is other than a boy nor that Burnett calling him "manly" strains against the evidence. Rather, he is definitely a boy whose character challenges the conventional distinctions between boys and girls as exemplified in the familiar nursery rhyme:

> *What are little boys made of?*
> *What are little boys made of?*

Frogs and snails
And puppy-dogs' tails,
That's what little boys are made of.

What are little girls made of?
What are little girls made of?
Sugar and spice
And all that's nice,
That's what little girls are made of.

Burnett was affirming, and thousands of mothers who dressed their boys in velvet agreed, that a boy who was thoughtful, kind, and considerate could still be as manly as any boy who played hooky from school or lit firecrackers in the house. (Jo March in Louisa May Alcott's *Little Women* [1868–1869] had already commenced challenging the wisdom of the rhyme on behalf of girls.)

Moreover, Burnett gave the model American boy a mother. Previously, admirable good boys—little George Washington or Rollo—were products of their fathers' molding. Without fathers and with the women left to govern them ineffectual, the admirable bad boys who were, after all, really good, such as Tom Bailey and Tom Sawyer, were free to act out their mischiefs and reveal their good-heartedness. But Burnett turned this around. Cedric's father, having played his necessary genealogical role, disappeared, leaving "Dearest" to form a good boy whose conduct stood in strong contrast to the bad behavior of the other Dorincourt males, while he, nevertheless, remained a boy.

American families were, after all, two-parent families, and although even in the latter decades of the nineteenth century they remained essentially patriarchal, nevertheless urban fathers, unlike rural fathers, left home for work daily, and boys who once grew up working alongside their fathers on farms now spent their days, in school and out, supervised by women. The underlying argument in *Little Lord Fauntleroy*, a fantasy of the overnight transformation of an American boy into an English lord, was that in the daily absence of fathers, mothers were responsible for the culture of the man-to-be. Little Cedric was able to step into the masculine role to which he had been called because, thanks to his mother, he was already gracious.

≡ AMERICA AS MIDDLE CLASS ≡

Adolescence, Frank Merriwell, Penrod

"The era of the adolescent," Joseph Kett wrote in his essential book on the subject, "dawned in Europe and America in the two decades after 1900."[1] Before that time adolescence had not been regarded as a stage of growth distinctly different in the nature of its concerns from either the childhood that preceded or the adulthood that followed it. Rather, it was a term applied to the years from, roughly speaking, the age of thirteen or fourteen to that of seventeen or eighteen. Those years when the boy developed into a man were regarded as a coherent stage in a continuing journey toward maturity. When Tocqueville noted that the boys in the United States he visited in 1831–1832 seemed to become men without this transitional period, he declared that in America there was no adolescence, an observation that may well have been affected by the fact that the American political system that he was studying also seemed not to have passed through an adolescent period in its movement from colonial dependency to independent nationhood. In the United States he visited, the major measure of manhood seemed to be neither age nor sexual development, but the position one held in the workplace. When a boy did a man's job he was a man.

Up to the closing decades of the nineteenth century, the United States was a nation of farms on which, indeed, the lives of boys seemed to elide adolescence. Charles Dudley Warner, who was an infant growing up on a farm in Western Massachusetts at the time of Tocqueville's American journey, recalled in his memoir, *Being a Boy* (1877), "Every boy is anxious to be a man and is very uneasy with the restrictions that are put upon him as a boy. Good fun as it is to yoke up the calves and play work, there is not a boy on a farm but would rather drive a yoke of oxen at real work."[2] Moreover, being a boy did not just mean not yet being a man, but, more distressingly, being numbered among the women: "Doing the regular work of the world is not much, the boy thinks, but the wearisome part is the waiting on the people who do that work. This is what the women and boys have to do, wait upon everybody who 'works.'"[3] Edginess at such gendered separation accelerated the boy's desire to tackle a man's job.

In his *Memoirs,* Ulysses S. Grant, born into an Ohio farm family in 1822, also described his transition from boy to man in terms of the work he did, and, in fond retrospect, made that transition appear seamless:

> When I was seven or eight years of age, I began hauling all the wood in the house and shops. I could not load it on the wagon of course at that time, but I would drive and the choppers would load and someone at the house unload. When about eleven years old I was strong enough to hold a plough. From that age until seventeen I did all the work done with horses, such as breaking up the land, furrowing, ploughing corn and potatoes, bringing in the crops when harvested, hauling all the wood, besides tending, two or three hours, a cow or two and sawing wood for stoves.[4]

Born in 1860, a generation after Warner and Grant, Hamlin Garland, in his reconstruction of his life on the family farm in Dry Run Prairie, Iowa, continues to represent the change from boy to man as an uninterrupted evolution; there was no classifiable period between being a boy and becoming a man. Adolescence was still a phase in an evolving whole rather than a distinct condition. Speaking of himself in the third person, because in writing about his experience he aimed at representing the condition of a generation of boys born on the prairie, Garland said: "He was a small edition of his father. He wore the same color and check in his hickory shirt, and his long pantaloons of blue denim had suspenders precisely like those of the men."[5] The boy did chores such as milking the cows, currying the horses, watering the cattle, and spreading fresh straw in the cows' stalls, and was pressed at an early age into running the plough team because the family could not afford a man to do the work. Although some observers found him too little for such arduous work, to him "This seemed like a fine and manly commission." Yet there was the hapless paradox of his entering upon a man's work with a boy's powerlessness: "Snowy mud gumming his boots making him groan in discomfort, he lost the sense of being a boy, yet he was unable to prove himself a man by quitting work."[6]

As a boy in harvest time Garland followed the binders who kept pace with the threshing machine, his task being to pick up the strays that escaped binding. Then at fifteen he became a binder, and "As the purring sickle [of the new McCormick Reaper] passed him and the angry rake delivered his first bundle to him with a jerk, his heart leaped. Right there he became a man." It was, he said, pretty much equivalent to being knighted.[7]

· · · · ·

The concept of adolescence as a stage of life markedly separate from what preceded it—a leap out of childhood but a landing short of adulthood—began to crystallize in the latter decades of the nineteenth century. In "The Moral and Religious Training of Children" in an 1882 *Princeton Review*, G. Stanley Hall, then a lecturer in the new field of psychology at Johns Hopkins University, described adolescence as a condition characterized by "lack of emotional steadiness, violent impulses, unreasonable conduct, lack of enthusiasm and sympathy. The previous selfhood is broken up . . . and a new individual is in the process of being born."[8] Two decades later, Hall, then president of Clark University, where he was establishing the leading American center for psychological study, published his lengthy study *Adolescence* (1904), a book of over 1,300 pages. In it he endorsed recapitulation theory and theorized that "adolescence corresponded to a period of prehistory marked by large-scale migrations."[9] Adolescence in boys, he said, is natural savagery. The social prohibition of premarital sex at an age when sexuality increases, the looming necessity of identifying an occupational position in order to assume financial responsibility, and the task of integrating tradition with newer ways of thinking pressed in upon the adolescent male, detaching him from his previous self.

With the recognition of the saltatory nature of adolescence came a widespread reconsideration of boyhood. No longer the fluid period of life exemplified in Tom Sawyer, who was a variety of ages until he was a man, or by Ulysses S. Grant, who moved from his boyhood into his manhood without a jolt, initial boyhood was now seen as a distinct stage that commenced in infancy to be terminated by the onset of adolescence, and psychologists focused on the best way for society to deal with troubled and potentially disruptive adolescents.

In addressing this problem, Hall drew heavily upon his own experience. Between the ages of nine and fourteen he had spent most of the time when his school was not in session with a farm family in Ashfield, Massachusetts, and his memory of life there led him to believe that where children are in great demand on the farm, "they are in a sense members of the firm. Evenings are not dangerous to morality, but are turned to good account, while during the rowdy or adolescent age the boyish tendency to savagery can find harmless vent in hunting, trapping, and other ways less injurious to morals than the customs of city life." He went on to speculate that the "heroes of '76" had come from circumstances such as those he observed in Ashfield, and to point out that such conditions were the direct reverse of those that prevailed in the South at the outbreak of the Civil War. The clear implication was that the North's military victory was also the victory of the ways of the New England farm family and that those ways should serve as a model of how contemporary society might counter the twinned threats of adolescence and urban life. Not unlike Charles Loring Brace, he added, "Should we ever have occasion to educate colonists, as England is now doing, we could not do better than by reviving conditions of life like these."[10]

If Tocqueville's contention that for American boys there was no adolescence seems connected to the fact that the United States itself came out of colonial dependency and into nationhood without a transitional period, Hall, with a new understanding of adolescence and its "savagery," seems in the latter part of the century to have anticipated the nation's imperial aspirations and put adolescence to their service.

But America was urbanizing, and, as David Macleod summarizes the matter in his history, while farm boys worked on the farm and poor city boys faced an urgent demand to bring home money, a growing number of middle-class city boys remained in junior and then high schools during their adolescence, and the spare time they had after school hours and in the summer was regarded as potentially dangerous:

Character builders troubled by teenage sensuality, weakness, and indiscipline concluded that they should prolong boyhood into the teens. After 1900, as concerns about teenagers crystallized around the new concept of adolescence, this desire to prolong boyhood became a central theme of character building. In effect, character builders proposed a trade. By remaining in school, middle-class boys had accepted prolonged dependency; now they should accept closer control in their spare time as well. In return adults would assure them of their masculinity and busy them with sports and outdoor ramblings, compensating the youth for loss of independence with a simulacrum of manliness.[11]

Monitored recreations, especially team sports, became a substitute for work, demanding, as they did, discipline. Tom Sawyer went fishing and swimming with other boys spontaneously and independently. Team sports were scheduled and regulated, requiring each boy to play a part in a whole supervised by adults.

· · · · ·

Walter Camp (b. 1859) was an outstanding athlete in his years at Yale, after which as a businessman and then coach he led the movement that transformed the international game of rugby into American football. Although it is a team sport, rugby nevertheless focuses on the individual who is carrying the ball, since no member of his team can run in advance of him. When he is tackled the game is not halted, and whatever regrouping takes place as a result takes place while play continues. The rule changes that Camp was prominent in developing established a static line of scrimmage at the beginning of each play from which teammates could move in advance of the ball carrier to interfere with those on the other side who were attempting to tackle him. When he was tackled, play was stopped until both teams lined up along the line of scrimmage again. This evolved into the practice of each individual on either side of the line of scrimmage being assigned a particular offensive or defensive role. Rugby, that is, became American football as each player carried out a specific assignment different from that of any other player on his team. A good team was praised for resembling a smooth-running machine.

In 1888 Camp selected the first All-American team, an exercise that has continued into the twenty-first century. Each member of the team is chosen because he is the best of all players nationwide at playing his particular position. Tom Sawyer may have been called an all-American boy because his thoughts and actions were typical of the thoughts and actions of all American boys. But the All-American in Camp's sense is not typical but superior, the best in America at performing the specific role he has been assigned. An All-American is one-eleventh of a whole.

· · · · ·

The most popular of the fictional heroes in the dawning era of team sports was Frank Merriwell, who appeared in Street and Smith's boys' magazine, *Tip Top Weekly* (slogan: "An Ideal Publication for the American Youth"), in the years 1896 to 1914. So large a following did the stories have that after their publication in the magazine they were quickly gathered, three or four at a time, into bound paperback books. Taken together, Merriwell material, a close student of their popularity estimated, takes the space of 208 novels of some eighty thousand words each.[12] Romping through the twenty thousand copies of the magazine that were distributed each week, Frank always led Yale to victory. But it was no easy matter, because kidnappers, illness, or some other calamity invariably kept him from the playing field for a good part of the game so that Yale's prospects always looked bleak until he escaped from the villains or rose from his sickbed to dash into the arena and score the winning points in the final moment of the game. Week after week, in story after story, Yale won, with Frank embodying the paradox of being a superhero without whom the team would surely lose, even as the narrative consistently affirmed that team play was the crucial element in success.

Characteristic of all Merriwell stories, "Frank Merriwell's High Jump," which appeared in the December 1, 1900, issue of *Tip Top Weekly*, furnishes the following maxims:

It takes a lot of hard work to win a place on any team and hold it.

The man who never does anything to develop himself physically and mentally can never expect to amount to much in the world.

The thing we got here [team play] . . . is the thing that is going to put us ahead when the real battle of life comes.

Team work is not different from the splendid working of a great machine.

Emphasizing the subordination of individual to organization, the narrative account of the game in that story is accompanied by two diagrams of the plays in the game, which summarize play in terms of organization rather than individual effort.

Of greatest significance in the world picture that the Merriwell stories presented for "the American Youth" was that Frank was not a boy, but a young man of college age, a prime example of what David Macleod in his study of character builders defined as an adolescence of prolonged boyhood. Frank has a girlfriend (rather unappetizingly named Inza Burrage), but there is, of course, no sexual, or even much of a romantic, relationship. Their connection is, rather, one of dependency and gallantry, Frank being called upon time and again to save Inza from certain death (the stories are too "pure" for her to be faced with a fate worse than death). When a mad dog was about to bite Inza, Frank, armed only with a clasp knife, fought the beast off; when she lay helpless on the rails before the onrushing afternoon express, Frank snatched her away in the nick of time. For these heroic acts Congress voted Frank a medal and Inza rewarded him with a kiss. But his work was never finished; shortly thereafter Inza managed to fall through the ice. A relationship based on such melodramatic recurrences fended off the sexual uncertainties that in the psychological literature of the day were beginning to be associated with adolescence, and, indeed, the very names of the girls in Frank's world acted as anaphrodisiacs: Inza's best friend was a "pretty girl" named Belinda Snodd.

But while it is irresistibly easy to make fun of the Merriwell stories—Frank should have known from the start, for instance, that men with black moustaches who wore capes were up to no good—the grand generalizations offered by their author, Gilbert Patten (who wrote under the pen name Burt L. Standish), were not unlike those that G. Stanley Hall, the expositor of adolescence as a psychological transformation, had arrived at in his praise of the morale of the Yankee farm, likening it to the Spirit of '76 and admiring the way in which farm boys became "part of the firm." Similarly, Patten summoned American history to endorse his picture of Frank Merriwell's world: "This was the America of our fathers, when it required no apology to be honest, courageous, and law abiding, when hard work was a prerequisite for success; when danger was to be confronted, not avoided, and duty was meant to be performed, not shirked."[13] What was shirked, however, was adolescence.

·　·　·　·　·

In the December 7, 1925, issue of *American Mercury*, the magazine he famously founded and edited together with H. L. Mencken, George Jean Nathan remarked of Standish (that is, Patten):

> I doubt in all seriousness if there was an American writer of twenty-five and thirty years ago who was so widely known and so widely read by the boys of his time. His readers numbered millions, and included all sorts of young men, rich and poor. For one who read Mark Twain's "Huckleberry Finn" or "Tom Sawyer," there were ten thousand who read Standish's "Frank Merriwell's Dilemma," . . . or "Frank Merriwell at Yale."[14]

With an easy self-confidence, Patten himself dismissed *Tom Sawyer* and *Huckleberry Finn*: "They were pretty good, but I couldn't get much real kick out of most juvenile literature."[15] And the piece about his writing that he published in the *Saturday Evening Post* (July 11, 1927) brimmed over with his sense of knowing how to do what other authors of juveniles never got quite right:

> When you're writing regular fiction, you draw your characters from life. But when you're writing for boys, you draw your characters from the imaginary world that boys live in. When I conceived Frank, I think I hit on approximately the boy that every kid would like to be. Not, mind you, the boy that every kid ought to be. That was the Horatio Alger idea, a moral in every story. But my boy pointed no moral; he was just every boy's ideal picture of himself.

He went on to say, "I have no reason to blush for the morals or ethics of the Merriwell stories. I did my best to keep them clean and make them beneficial without allowing them to become namby-pamby or Horatio Algerish."[16]

Yet if the Frank Merriwell stories are devoid of the won-
ders and anxieties that visited Tom and Huck or the material
concerns that inhabited the working lives of Ragged Dick and
his companions, they do, nevertheless, advance their own
social agenda as surely as did Alger's stories. The sublima-
tion of adolescent rebelliousness into one's obligations to the
team was a paradigm of patriotic duty, as the historian John
Higham makes clear:

> We are well aware of the aggressive nationalism that
> sprang up after 1890. We do not so often notice analo-
> gous ferments in other spheres, [such as] . . . a boom in
> sports. . . . The link between the new athleticism and the
> new jingoism was especially evident in the yellow press.
> William Randolph Hearst's *New York Journal* created the
> modern sports page in 1896, just when its front page filled
> with atrocity stories of the bloody debauchery of Spanish
> brutes in Cuba.[17]

The Spanish-American War was played out before the public as an invigorating team sport, and even after World War I
had chastened such glorification, Frank Merriwell hung on,
assisted by the expanding popularity of college sports. He
reappeared in comic books and then, in 1934, a radio serial,
before disappearing entirely when the world went to war
again.[18] Alger we still have with us, commerce always manag-
ing to trump war.

· · · · ·

In the first decades of the twentieth century, adolescence
accelerated its detachment from boyhood. For a growing
number of middle-class American boys, the years of school
attendance were stretching past childhood, and with their
attendance in junior high and then high schools, students

were being separated into grades that, in effect, placed them in social as well as academic groups defined by birth dates. Previously, in the one-room schoolhouse and its modified successors, boys of different ages shared the same classroom, and having thus spent their school time together also mingled in their activities outside the school. The cultural shift exemplified by the new, essentially urban organization of the school converted Tom Sawyer and his kind into icons of a revered American past. The representative American boy of the twentieth century was to come from a middle-class urban family, his narrative an unapologetic exposition of its values even as those values were being assailed in prominent literary works of the 1910s and '20s.[19] That boy's name was Penrod.

The title character of *Penrod* (1914) is a boy of twelve living in a midsize Midwestern American city, very much like the Indianapolis in which its author, Booth Tarkington, was born in 1869, and to which he returned to live in 1911 after having moved between the United States and Europe during the years in which he won his initial fame as both novelist and playwright. *The Gentleman from Indiana* (1899), the first of his novels to be published, was so large a success that his publisher claimed it made Tarkington the most famous man in America, and the first of his plays, *The Man from Home* (1908), which he cowrote, ran for five years on Broadway. To his death in 1946 Tarkington continued to compose in both genres at a prodigious rate. He wrote plays for such eminent actors as Alfred Lunt, Billie Burke, and Helen Hayes, and twice won the Pulitzer Prize for his novels: *The Magnificent Ambersons* (1918) and *Alice Adams* (1921). In all, he wrote more than thirty novels, as well as numerous short stories and occasional works of nonfiction.

Tarkington's achievement is astounding, not just because of the number of his works, but also because of their superior craftsmanship and the influence his mastery of the self-contained episode had upon the structure of the emerging forms of mass entertainment, radio and then television serials. He excelled in the creation of plots based on a continuing character whose story consisted of separate, self-contained episodes, each complete in itself, rather than on incidents linked causally to form a whole made up of a beginning, middle, and end. *Penrod* is a model of the technique.[20]

Twelve-year-old Penrod Schofield has a mother, father, and older sister. Theirs is the two-parent family that in much of the twentieth-century literature about boys replaced the one-parent (or proxy) families of Tom Bailey, Tom Sawyer, Ragged Dick, and Cedric Errol. Although the daily supervision of Penrod is the responsibility of his mother, his misdemeanors are referred for punishment to his father upon his return home from work, and both parents and son unquestioningly assume that the awaited punishment will be physical.

"Mothers must accept the fact that between boyhood and manhood their sons do not boast of them," Tarkington writes in *Penrod*. "'Your mother won't let you,' is an insult. But 'My father won't let me,' is a dignified explanation and cannot be hooted." The family dynamic is summarized by Penrod's ninety-year-old great-aunt when she says his parents don't know what to do with him, because his mother thinks he is a novice in a convent and is disappointed in him whenever he doesn't behave like one, while his father believes he is a decorous, well-trained young businessman, and whenever he doesn't live up to that standard he is "walloped." Tarkington himself held to the recapitulation theory. "I began to see that just as in his embryo man reproduces the history of his development upward from the mire into man, so does he in his childhood and his boyhood and his youth reproduce the onward history of his race, from the most ancient man to the most modern."[21]

The actual scrapes Penrod gets into, however, are only in a superficial sense primitive. In the main they are comical failures to do what is required of him at home, in school, or at play. A good deal of that comic effect derives from the fact that author and reader share the knowledge that little boys cannot be cured of being little boys except by growing up, while Penrod's exasperated elders are, nevertheless, taxed with the responsibility of seeing that he comports himself otherwise.

Disturbingly, however, Tarkington's adherence to the belief that boyhood is a reproduction of the precivilized condition of mankind leads to Penrod's being insensible of the feeling of others. Aunt Polly said of Tom Sawyer, "He never meant any harm and he was the best-hearted boy that ever was." Serena Harper said it was the same with her Joe, who was "always full of devilment and up to every mischief, but he was just as unselfish and kind as he could be." But that "bad boy" has disappeared. Penrod lacks any instinct for the emotional life of others, and Tarkington, relying on the reader's acceptance of the premise that boys are by nature indifferent to the sensibility of others, converts the consequences of his ignorant indifference into comedy. From another perspective, however, such indifference might well be regarded as, at the very least, callousness.

· · · · ·

Constantly interfering with his sister's and her suitor's attempts at privacy unless bribed to desist, Penrod originated American domestic comedy's convention of the annoying little brother. Tarkington, in effect, announced the fact: "The serious poetry of all languages had omitted the little brother, and yet he is one of the great trials of love—the immemorial burden of courtship." But at the same time, Penrod does have his Becky Thatcher in Marjorie Jones, who, in the novel's closing scene, a birthday party for his twelfth year, pulls him by the ear away from another girl with whom he is dancing too closely. Although he obeys her, Penrod doesn't understand why Marjorie behaves that way, or, for

Penrod and Marjorie Jones

that matter, why he acquiesces, but Marjorie knows full well, and, Tarkington comments, "He was precisely in the condition of an elderly spouse detected in flagrant misbehaviour." The novel thus concludes with a tacit assurance that for all his wildness Penrod is indeed heading toward civilization as defined by the Schofield family's way of life. The dances and other social affairs that his truculent resistance amusingly disrupts are markers of his family's middle-class values, and to recognize the true worth of that culture, Tarkington implies, one need only consider what the alternative would be. Although *Penrod* is a novel about a middle-class white boy growing up in a society of his peers, it contains a remarkable number of scenes involving Negroes, all of them denigrating. Penrod's "savagery" is an early stage of his journey toward culture, but it is only a stage. The Negro characters illustrate what it means to be arrested at that stage and how nice it is, after all, to be a Schofield.

Victorine, a girl in Penrod's class, is an "octoroon"—Tarkington so characterizing her in apparent explanation of why she is in the same school as middle-class white children—and she happens to sit in front of Penrod, who "hates" her. No reason for this is given. Rather, in his boredom Penrod dips her ribbon-bound braid into his inkwell so that when she leans forward her clean, white blouse is smudged. The episode is not developed beyond that act, but exists simply to demonstrate that Penrod is bored in school and has found an amusing way to alleviate the tedium. But one may further reflect that in darkening her blouse Penrod had found a way of reminding Victorine who she really was.

Next to his friend Sam Williams, Penrod's closest daily playmates are Herman and Verman, Negro boys who live in the alley behind his house where the family stable is located. They are regular participants in one or another of Penrod's playtime projects, at times taking part in them only reluctantly. For example, when Penrod demands that they perform as scantily clad savages in a play he puts on for the neighborhood children, advertising them as wild men whose father is in jail, they protest before giving in. But they always do finally yield to Penrod's demands (or his bribery), their friendly but submissive relationship mirroring the pattern of race relations in the Schofields' America. Tarkington himself has no doubts about the propriety, indeed the necessity, of such subservience. Describing Herman and Verman, he calls them "the not very remote descendants of Congo man-eaters." Although less flagrant, other detrimental remarks about Negro behavior recur from time to time to frame the world in which Penrod is situated; for example, "Penrod was doing something very unusual and rare, something almost never accomplished except by coloured people or by a boy in school on a spring day; he was really doing nothing at all."

In an extraordinary, perhaps the most extraordinary, episode in the book, class difference is distinguished from racial difference when Penrod strikes up an acquaintance with Rupe Collins, who is from the other part of town—his father works in a factory. Rupe is bigger than Penrod and physically dominates him, twisting his arm, forcing him to the ground to "eat dirt," and time and again luring him into a position of seeming comradeship only again to punish him physically. But Penrod is fascinated. Never before had he met such an impressively rough and tough character, and in their meetings he submits to whatever pummeling Rupe administers in the glory of being admitted to his company and the hope of becoming just like him. Among his friends and family he practices Rupe's postures, assuming a vocal swagger that astounds his classmates and baffles his family at the dinner table. Rupe is from the city's Third School District, and the menacing warning he often issues to Penrod is "you'd last just about one day up at the Third," a warning Penrod, in turn, is fond of issuing to his baffled friends at school, who know that Penrod has never been "up at the Third."

*"Yes, sonny, Rupe Collins is my name, and you
better look out what you say when he's around!"*

One day, intending to bask in the aura of Rupe's friendship, Penrod arranges to show off his newfound associate to Sam, Herman, and Verman, on an afternoon when Rupe has condescended to be at the stable where the boys regularly meet. There the bullying Rupe makes the mistake of calling Herman a "nig," at which little Verman hits him from behind with a rake, because "in his simple, direct African way he wished to kill his enemy, and he wished to kill him as soon as possible." In the ensuing fight, the Negro boys trounce Rupe, who "had not learned that an habitually aggressive person runs the danger of colliding with beings in one of the lower stages of evolution wherein theories about 'hitting below the belt' have not yet made their appearance." Thoroughly battered by Herman and Verman, Rupe makes his escape, never to be seen in that part of town again, and Penrod emerges from the incident purged of admiration for him.

Although he orders Herman and Verman about and treats them as inferiors, Penrod never called them "nig," and they, performing their role in the hierarchy of their society, accept his authority. But when a boy from the other part of town, which is to say from the working class, insults and presumes to command them, they are outraged. Rupe forgot his place, and in affirming a difference that Penrod failed to recognize, Herman and Verman restored him to his class.

The Rupe Collins episode is the fullest and most explicit dramatization of social differences in the novel, but there are other, quieter distinctions that also point up the middle-class, mid-American center of the novel's social values. For example, Maurice Levy, a boy in Penrod's school, is numbered among his friends and serves also as an occasional irritant, since it is he whom Marjorie selects to be seen with in the moments when she feels the need to cure Penrod of his inattention. But it is also obvious that, finally, Maurice, who wears a pearl pin in his tie and boasts that his costume for the pageant was made by the best tailor in town, does not quite fit in.

The costumes of the others were made by mothers and sisters, not, of course, from financial necessity but because that was the unobtrusive way such things were done. And a pearl pin! Maurice and his mother still have some way to go before they can even hope to belong to the Schofields' society, as they might have realized had they read Edith Wharton's *The House of Mirth* (1905). In this respect, *Penrod* seems a middle-class reduction of the class standards exhibited in that novel.

The large and warm reception *Penrod* received from readers encouraged Tarkington to write two sequels: *Penrod and Sam* and *Penrod Jashber*, both made up of stories that had been serialized in magazines from 1915 onward before they appeared in book form. In them, the racial theme continued to flow as a powerful undercurrent in excess of any demand the plot placed upon it. In *Penrod and Sam*, Penrod locks Verman in his sister Margaret's closet, then forgets him when other matters attract his attention. Verman thus remains shut up in the dark for hours in order to serve the comic purpose of frightening Margaret when she opens the door and he bolts out. Whether he had been frightened is not known. In another episode, Verman is forced to surrender his only pair of trousers, just altered by his mother from an old pair of his older brother Herman's, because Penrod and Sam had commandeered Herman's trousers in order to lengthen a line they were lowering into the well. Herman protested, without avail as usual, and then Penrod and Sam quite predictably proceeded to lose the trousers down the well, forcing Herman to reclaim the pair of his outgrown trousers from Verman, who then had to tag along home in his underwear. Both are in fear of how their mother, who had spent the previous night cutting and reshaping the trousers, will react to their condition, but we do not follow them into their home. Rather, we learn that Penrod and Sam "sympathized with Herman," but they regarded the trousers as a "loss about which there was no use in making such an outcry."

· · · · ·

With *Seventeen* (1916), another popular novel—it went "through various dramatic versions . . . silent movie, stage play, musical comedy, talking movie, and again in 1951, a new musical"[22]—Tarkington moved on to the portrayal of adolescence. The novel consists of episodes in Will ("Silly Billy") Baxter's attempt to win the favor of a belle of his age who is visiting the city for the summer and has smitten every boy in his circle with her atrocious baby talk. In a fine tactical move, Tarkington ingeniously creates a commonsense counter to the vapid belle, not in another adolescent girl of her age, but in Will's clear-minded nine-year-old sister, Jane, whose perception of reality is much more astute than that of Will and his fellow adolescents. In her shrewd innocence, Jane appears far more attractive than Penrod or any of his companions had been in their "savagery." Girls, apparently, had already arrived at the goal of civilization and so were exempt from having to recapitulate the historical steps that led up to it as boys were required to do.

Seventeen is the story of an awkward adolescent in the comic pangs of first love. When the critic Heywood Broun complained that the author should have tried "to capture some of the torments that come to the young through their first recognition of sex," Tarkington replied, "I never knew a youth who had that sense of torment under the circumstances depicted in 'Seventeen.'"[23] The popularity of *Seventeen* seems connected to this adherence to the belief that sexual anxiety and its concomitant frustrations are not necessarily a part, or at least are not necessarily a remembered part, of teenage romance. *Seventeen*, that is, held the twentieth century at bay, and its popularity indicated that was the way many chose to remember their own teen years.

Looking back at 1900 from his perspective in 1928, Tarkington wrote, "There was a tremendous respect for respectability," which "did not make the town gloomy; and looking back at it now, it seems to have been not only a contented and peaceful place but a fairly happy one."[24] Such peace and happiness formed the ambience of the many stories of middle-class American life that followed Tarkington's lead in popular fiction, both on the page and on the stage. As years passed, the blatant racism of *Penrod*, which had been carried into *Seventeen* as well as the other Penrod stories, slowly softened in the fictions for which they can be seen to have served as prototypes. Yet the prejudice was still there in the comic and lazy (but no longer barbaric) Negro characters. Retaining their auxiliary position, those from the other side of the tracks came to appear less menacing than Rupe had been, and characters whose names and accents bore strong ethnic markings began to make their appearance as (frequently comic) acquaintances, even friends, of the protagonist, but not as his social equals.

As the twentieth century advanced, the adjective "American" came increasingly to mean middle-class, and with it the ground of exclusion from the fraternity of the all-American boy shifted from character to social background. Even the son of the vicious town drunk had been included in Tom Sawyer's gang. Those who were kept out were not of a different class but a different character—they were prigs. But neither lower-class Ragged Dick nor noble Cedric Errol was so disconnected from the fellowship of boys from another class as was Penrod Schofield, his popularity a testimony to Tarkington's skill in portraying respectability as the signal virtue of American life.

Like Tom Sawyer, however, Penrod, too, had a rich imagination, and while Tom, influenced by his reading in tales of the Arabian Nights or the deeds of the Knights of the Round Table, converted the everyday reality of a Sunday school excursion into an exotic caravan, Penrod, influenced by his reading in the dime literature of the Old West, took out pencil and paper in his hideaway in the barn and worked intermittently on his saga of "Harold Ramorez, the Roadagent." If, anticipating that Tom might very well disappear into the conventions of middle-class American life if he were allowed to mature, Twain concluded his story before Tom left boyhood, this does not deny that there is more than a trace of the adult Tom Sawyer in Mark Twain's numerous business ventures. Still, the literary master is distinguishable from the businessman. There is a closer connection between Penrod and his author.

Mark Twain left Hannibal before his literary career had begun, and when he turned to it as a literary source he did so from his writing desks in Hartford and Elmira. Tarkington, on the other hand, returned to live in his native Indianapolis, where he had located Penrod in endorsement of the way of life he valued and summed up in the word "respectable." Penrod and his successors were participants in Tarkington's historical present. So long as the class values and prejudices they embodied were widely shared, they were looked to as exemplary American boys. When, however, their infrastructure of class and racial discrimination began to crumble, they crumbled with it. But even at the moment of his arrival, Tom Sawyer was already an historical figure, the boy who would outlive the small-mindedness of provincial America, yet bring to its industrialized successor the character and skills nurtured by village life. Preserved in the amber of his matchless moment, he remains the all-American boy.

≡ ANTITHESES ≡

Huckleberry Finn, Holden Caulfield

lthough Huckleberry Finn's character proved to be the very antithesis of Tom Sawyer's, his narrative made its initial appearance (English edition 1884, American 1885) riding on Tom's coattails. *Adventures of Huckleberry Finn* carried the subtitle *(Tom Sawyer's Comrade)*, and the illustration on the cover of the American edition pictured Huck standing in front of a whitewashed fence. It was a prop borrowed from Tom's novel; no such fence appeared in Huck's. And while few if any of the incensed contemporary critics of *Huckleberry Finn* cited *Tom Sawyer* in contrast, their indignation at what they regarded as a coarse narrative with parts that came perilously close to outright immorality may well have been provoked by the discovery of how opposite the new novel was to its pleasing predecessor. Mark Twain, it seemed to them, had misplaced whatever small literary skill he had once possessed.

Tom Sawyer had been narrated by an adult author who was at a considerable remove from Tom himself, but *Huckleberry Finn* was turned over to Huck to tell the tale in the only language he possessed. It was ungrammatically colloquial, with images drawn from the experience of a boy who had lived his life at the bottom of society in a village on the banks of the Mississippi, the river's majestic presence a constant comment upon the banality of the life that bordered it. The adults with whom he was acquainted were either illiterate and superstitious or well meaning but disconcertingly self-righteous, and he was far more comfortable with the former than with the latter, bent, as they were, on raising him from the rough circumstances in which he was contentedly situated to a life of stringently defined propriety. Had he accepted their discipline, they would have refined his diction and provided his narrative with the stock of tried, true, and tired literary images of which it was refreshingly deprived. He would have learned, for example, that there was a far more civilized way to describe the professional demeanor of an undertaker than to say "he had no more smile than a ham." What made such locutions irritating, in the view of the novel's foes, was not just that they were "unliterary," but that, unfortunately, they actually succeeded in doing their job. One got the picture immediately.

Although notable characters in fiction, David Copperfield, for example, begin their stories by providing accounts of their boyhood, no novel in English had ever had as its narrator a boy who remained a boy throughout. Unmediated by adult experience, the clear-sighted, unsophisticated immediacy of Huck's encounters with those who were noble yet murderous, comic yet criminal, tenderhearted yet narrow-minded, challenged social and religious convictions, not because Huck himself satirized them, but because aware of his base social position and lack of book learning, he woefully concluded that the disturbing discrepancies he noticed between proclaimed standards of conduct and the behavior of the individuals who proclaimed them could probably be explained by those who possessed the learning he lacked. He was sure, for example, that Tom Sawyer, who had schooling and a good upbringing, would be able to reconcile what he in his ignorance saw as inconsistencies, such as that between the conduct of those who professed piety and the content of the piety they professed. His failure to understand why religious belief became all the more necessary at precisely those moments when all else, even prayer, seemed to fail amounted to an "irreverence" that sorely vexed the novel's opponents, who attacked Huck's character and language but were unable or unwilling themselves to address the discrepancies that troubled him. His character being dismissed, his observations could be ignored, and this continued to be the tactic of the novel's opponents into the twentieth century. *Huckleberry Finn* ranks fifth in the American Library Association's list of the "100 Most Frequently Challenged Books: 1990–2000," a testimony to its persisting power to disturb; the four books that precede it on the list were published between 1969 and 1991.[1]

A hint of contentions to come was provided by Richard Watson Gilder, editor of the *Century* magazine, who was eager to have the novel make its first appearance as a serial in his pages. Although Twain was resolute in his contention that such an appearance would damage the sale of the novel when it appeared in book form, he knew that many a popular novel had first made its appearance as a magazine serial, and it is probable that, recognizing the kind of editorial changes that would have to be made to suit the magazine's conception of its genteel readership, he was unwilling to permit the entire novel to undergo such revision. Selections, on the other hand, could be altered to suit the magazine's editorial practice, then restored when the novel appeared as a book. Accordingly, the *Century* did publish selections that were, with Twain's consent, sanitized by its editors. In the *Century*, for example, Huck's statement that Jim and he were "always naked day and night, whenever the mosquitoes would let us," was omitted, as were such figurative indelicacies as the image of Pap's room after a drunken night: "they had to take soundings before they could navigate it."[2]

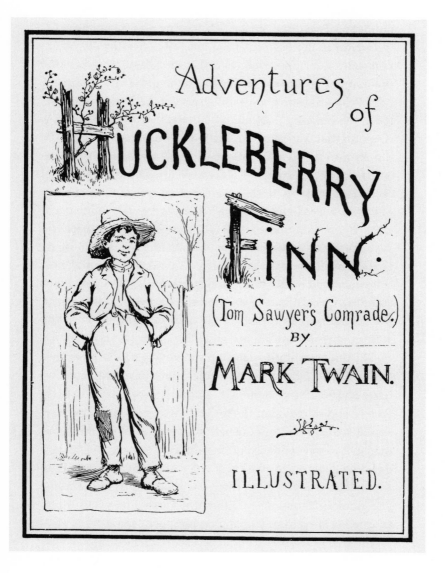

Adventures
of
HUCKLEBERRY
FINN.
(Tom Sawyer's Comrade.)

BY

MARK TWAIN.

ILLUSTRATED.

Title page of the first edition of Huckleberry Finn

Gilder's tepid gentility was, however, only a pale fore-shadowing of what followed immediately after the book was published. Even the *Century*'s tinkering was insufficient for the writer in the *Boston Herald* who after reading the magazine selections observed (February 1, 1885), "It is pitched in but one key, and that is the key of a vulgar and abhorrent life." When the book was published and the library committee of the Concord Public Library voted not to circulate it—a decision that was to be duplicated by one or another public library into the twentieth century—one member of the Concord committee explained: "I have examined the book and my objections to it are these: it deals with a series of adventures of very low grade morality; it is couched in the language of a rough ignorant dialect; and all through its pages there is a systematic use of bad grammar and an employment of rough, coarse, inelegant expressions. It is also very irreverent." Lest the equivalence of sound literary principles to social-class standing was still not clear, the explanation concluded with the outright declaration that the book was "More fit for the slums than for respectable people."[3]

The Concord library decision was widely cited, sometimes derisively by the novel's advocates, but more often approvingly by those who endorsed similar proscriptions in their locales and relied upon the force their argument for censorship would derive from the hallowed position Concord occupied in Americans' sense of their literary culture. No literary decision could have attracted wider national attention than that of the committee in the town that had been the home of Emerson, Thoreau, and Margaret Fuller, and where Hawthorne, residing in its Old Manse, had spent some of his most productive years. In historical perspective, the Concord decision not to circulate *Huckleberry Finn* seems a sad descent from the cultural confidence of the age of Emerson to a nervous defense of the eminence he had won for a town that now felt itself threatened by a growing immigrant population

within it and the redefinition of national culture emerging from the expanding population of the West. Unwittingly, the Concord committee had illustrated the validity of Emerson's assertion that the healthy attitude of human nature manifested in the behavior of boys became lost in the conformity society demanded of them as they grew older; that, in effect, society everywhere is "in conspiracy against the manhood of every one of its members." During his lecture tour to the West in January 1856, Emerson had actually been exhilarated by his exposure to local manners, and after a "stout Illinoisan" walked out of one of his lectures he returned to his room to observe in his notebook: "The architect who is asked to build a ship to go upon the sea must not build a parthenon or a square house, but a ship. . . . I must give my wisdom a comic form instead of tragics or elegaics."[4] This suggests more sympathy with the Mark Twain who was yet to be than with what the custodians of culture in Concord would become.

So vehement were the novel's opponents that their reaction at the time of its appearance received greater attention than the respectable number of favorable and highly perceptive reviews that also accompanied its publication. Nevertheless, in the days following the publication of *Huckleberry Finn* the ground began silently shifting from under the all-American boy, although his demise was more than a half-century away.

$\bullet \;\; \bullet \;\; \bullet \;\; \bullet \;\; \bullet$

Upon the English publication of *Huckleberry Finn*, Mark Twain's friend the literary critic Brander Matthews wrote in London's *Saturday Review*, "The skill with which the character of Huck Finn is maintained is marvelous. We see everything through his eye and not a pair of Mark Twain's spectacles. . . . one of the most artistic things in *Huckleberry Finn* is the sober self-restraint with which Mr. Clemens lets

Huck Finn set down, without any comment at all, scenes which would have afforded the ordinary writer matter for endless moral and political and sociological disquisition."[5]

While Matthews's remarks centered on the literary achievement of the novel, influential praise of its moral and historical importance came from Franklin Sanborn, whose argument, trenchant in itself, gained increased strength from the fact that he had been an important participant in the intellectual life of Concord in its glory days. Born in 1831 in New Hampshire, Sanborn had moved to Concord, where in 1854 he established the school to which Emerson sent his children, and with Emerson he was one of the founders of the Transcendental Movement. His passionate support of John Brown had led federal marshals to attempt to arrest and convey him to Washington to testify about his part in the Harper's Ferry raid, but they were foiled by the shielding citizens of Concord. After the Civil War, Sanborn entered upon a distinguished career of social activism and literary achievement. He wrote biographies of Emerson, Bronson Alcott, and Thoreau, and edited Thoreau's letters, while performing a central part in the founding of institutions such as the Massachusetts Infant Asylum, the Clarke Institution for the education of the deaf, and the American Social Science Organization. His defense of *Huckleberry Finn* appeared in the Springfield *Republican* (April 1885), a newspaper that editorially had sided with those who condemned the novel. He was at the time inspector of charities in the Commonwealth of Massachusetts.

Brushing past the superficiality of the many attacks on the novel's coarseness and unsuitability for young or genteel readers, Sanborn addressed its moral significance and spoke of it as a work of major historical importance. Had the critics no memory of the place and the time in which the novel was set? "As a picture of Missouri life and manners it is simply invaluable, and goes farther to explain the political history of the United States from 1854 to 1860 than any other work I have seen."

Noting that "there is hardly anything so true to human nature in the whole realm of casuistry as the young hero's meditations with himself over his duty regarding the runaway slave Jim, when it first dawns upon the boy that he is an accomplice," Sanborn emphasized the importance of *Huckleberry Finn* as a major moral as well as historical document. His friend Thoreau had famously placed individual conscience above law when he went to jail for withholding taxes from a state that was in complicity with slaveholding states, and Sanborn saw the principle that led to Thoreau's civil disobedience displayed fictionally in Huck's conduct. He did not explicitly liken Twain's Huck to Thoreau, but his appreciation of Huck's actions placed Huck in the distinguished company of those who in their day had refused on principle to comply with legalized injustice. He saw *Huckleberry Finn* as a major American work not just because it established American speech as a potent literary medium, but because it attached that speech to the history of nonconformity. Implicit in Sanborn's own career of political protest, as well as in his praise of *Huckleberry Finn*, is his valuing of the part dissent played in American history: the New England colonies had been founded upon nonconformity with the established church, and the American Revolution had resulted from refusal to conform with legal impositions. If the all-American boy such as Tom Sawyer was representative of the United States as a whole, it did not follow that Huck Finn, his antithesis, was anti-American. Rather, he sounded an equally American counterpoint to the dominant theme.

In concluding his argument, Sanborn struck a slyly anticlimactic note somewhat remindful of Twain's manner: "Though the Concord committee have banished the book itself as immoral, I can see nothing worse in it than the story of Samson, which contains a great deal of deliberate lying, or the story of Noah, which has a good deal about drinking, rafting and high water."[6]

· · · · ·

The literary history of the all-American boy is marked by the prominence of the "bad" boy's superiority to the "good" boy; by, that is, the recognition that daring Tom Sawyer, not his compliant brother Sid, is the boy whom American society awaits and will reward. It rests confidently upon the belief that such a valuation is desirable, because for all its imperfections America, like the all-American boy himself, is morally justified. What was deeply troubling about *Huckleberry Finn*—ever present to its critics but suppressed in their more facile assaults on Huck's character—was the moral portrait of America itself that emerged. Although the novel vigorously attacked the institution of slavery, that institution had been abolished some twenty year before the novel appeared and was not an issue in its reception. More to the point, however, the novel challenged national faith in the grandeur of the American character, as was, for example, comfortably available in *Little Lord Fauntleroy*, published in the following year. Although there were, to be sure, villainous persons in Huck's narrative, they, Pap, or the Duke and Dauphin, were, at bottom, as comic as they were threatening. It was, rather, the depiction of the actions of the good people that truly troubled. The kindly woman who penetrates Huck's disguise as a girl and tells him that if he ever gets into trouble "You send word to Mrs. Judith Loftus, which is me, and I'll do what I can to get you out of it" sits at home anticipating the reward for Jim's capture that will be earned by her husband, who is out slave-catching; the courtly Grangerfords, who welcome the orphaned Huck into their home, are engaged in a homicidal, self-annihilating feud over an issue that no one can clearly call to mind; citizens outraged by the autocratic

Colonel Sherburn steps out to confront the mob.

Colonel Sherburn's cold-blooded murder of the harmless town drunk are derisively faced down by him in demonstration of his claim that "the average man's a coward"; tenderhearted Aunt Sally, hearing that a steamboat explosion killed "only" a Negro, says, "Well, it's lucky, because sometimes people do get hurt." It is not the scoundrels and drunkards but such people who make up the "sivilization" from which Huck at novel's end flees into the wilds of the Indian Territory.

· · · · ·

M any have seen Holden Caulfield of *The Catcher in the Rye* (1951), who also tells his tale in the idiom of boys of his age and class, as the twentieth-century heir of Huck Finn. An instant success upon its publication, *Catcher* was adopted by the Book-of-the-Month Club, but unlike almost all other novels that have profited from that selection, it maintained its popularity and its influence beyond the days of initial enthusiasm. "Ten years after the first publication, over a million and a half copies had been sold in the United States," it had been translated into dozens of languages, and it was on the reading lists of many high schools, even in Europe.[7] The book's sales received the further stimulus of its being banned by school districts in Louisville, Tulsa, and San Jose because of its "foul language," a complaint more easily substantiated and self-righteously championed than censorship on moral or political grounds could be, although such concerns certainly drove the verbal fussiness. The same kind of complaint, reinforced by an insistence upon proper grammar, had been leveled at the far less popular *Huckleberry Finn* upon its publication. As Pamela Hunt Steinle writes in her analysis of the controversies that surrounded the novel's reception, "*Catcher* had the dubious distinction of being at once the most frequently censored book across the country and the second most frequently taught novel in the public schools."[8] Going on to survive the kind of instant fame that in most cases is followed by a precipitous descent, *The Catcher in the Rye* mellowed into distinction as a modern classic.

Holden Caulfield is seventeen looking back on his six-teen-year-old self when he speaks of the time in the previous December when he left his Pennsylvania prep school in anticipation of the formal expulsion he was about to receive, and spent a few days wandering in New York before confronting his parents with the news of his dismissal. Holden is some four years older than Huck was when he began his raft journey, but, he tells us, "Sometimes I can act like I was twelve,"

and like Huck he is as yet too innocent to come to terms
with the inequities, even the iniquitousness, of the world he
encounters. Like Huck, he survives in his world by lying, and
does so with detailed embellishments that suggest his taking
an aesthetic relish in the act. Huck lies to maintain his and
Jim's independence from the controls society would impose
upon them, conformity in his case, slavery in Jim's. Holden
lies to protect his constantly threatened sense that he is different from the "phonies," all those whom he sees as having
been compromised by society. The counterfeit selves he takes
on in conversations with strangers—that he must, for example, undergo an operation for a brain tumor—while false, are
not "phony," because he knows when he does so that he is
fabricating, whereas the phonies he loathes actually believe
themselves to be the false persons they represent themselves
as being. Yet even as his lies serve his desire to keep reality at
bay, they are tinged with the recognition that reality is bound
all too soon to break through. When finally overtaken by what
he opposed, Huck fled outward into the continental wilder-
ness; similarly overtaken, Holden retreats inward toward
an incipient madness that is the "Indian Territory" of post-
Hiroshima America.

Huck's adventures took place principally outdoors; Hold-
en's are indoors. The sequence of confined spaces he occupies
in his journey from Pencey Prep into Manhattan—railroad
carriage, taxis, nightclub, hotel room, bedroom closet, and a
couch that is too short for him in the disheveled living room
of the Antolinis—is the outward representation of a mental
secession that will culminate in the enclosure of a hospital
room. The nuns he admires carried innocence into adulthood
in a manner unavailable to him, as his futile attempts to erase
graffiti from the school walls indicate. Adulthood's approach
is relentless. Huck's movement down the Mississippi and his
eventual disappearance into the West constituted a crossing of geographic boundaries into the social and physical

boundlessness of the West. But Holden's journey is toward home and steadily increasing confinements.

Despite the hypocrisies and homicides he had witnessed in the communities through which he had passed on his journey down the river,[9] Huck believed that there was something right about the world of Tom Sawyer and something wrong about his inability to adapt to it. His narrative is grounded on that irony. Yet so also is his freedom, because without his acceptance of the rightness of Tom's world and his own unfitness for it, he would have been confronted with the responsibility of coping with the wrongs he perceived rather than taking flight from them. Holden, on the other hand, both contemning his contemporaries yet not believing it possible for them to be other than they are, retreats from conflict with them while remaining in their world. His passivity has led one critic to contend that "the culture's emphasis on 'winning' in encounters with other people is so threatening to him that he plays it safe by always losing."[10] But Holden's "playing safe" is the creation of an author who on D-Day had landed on a Normandy beach with a regiment of 3,800 members, only 1,300 of whom survived to war's end, had fought in the Battle of the Bulge, and had participated in the liberation of Dachau, serving as an interpreter for survivors of that horror. J. D. Salinger had his own views about "winning," and said that he "hated Hemingway's 'overestimation' of sheer physical courage, commonly called 'guts,' as a virtue."[11] Different as *The Catcher in the Rye* is from Hemingway's *The Sun Also Rises* (1926), it is also a determinedly postwar novel.

Holden's "tragedy," William Faulkner observed, was that "when he attempted to enter the human race there was no human race there."[12] The same might be said of Huck, but Huck had a place to go.

· · · · ·

Tom Sawyer and Huck Finn were companions, sharing the same time and place, each with room in that America to pursue his own kind of happiness. They complemented one another. But Tom's successor, Penrod, had no such complementary companion, and for all the difference between Penrod's moral opacity and Holden's acute sensitivity, Holden, who in noted ways resembles Huck, is in class, knowledge, and social confidence much closer to Penrod.

The Catcher in the Rye brims over with Holden's contented awareness of his social status. Whatever academic authority Mr. Spencer, his instructor, possesses, for example, is clearly nullified by Holden's distaste for Spencer's shabby material surroundings. Similarly, his toying with the ignorance of the vacationing office workers in the nightclub is a conscious exercise of his class as well as his intellectual superiority— they don't even know the difference between the second-rate nightclub they are in and the El Morocco!—and he pays for their drinks (although they should at least have offered to do so) in a further assertion of class difference and its basis in wealth. "The thing is," as Holden remarks, "it's really hard to be roommates with people if your suitcase is much better than theirs."

Whether or not we (or he) like it, sympathetic Holden Caulfield shares more with Penrod Schofield than with Huckleberry Finn. To note this is neither to disparage him nor to recuperate Penrod, but simply to identify Holden's right relation to the family of all-American boys. In a desperate moment he had imagined an escape to a cabin in the Maine woods, its manifest impossibility an indication that he was not Huck nor was his America that of Tom Sawyer. Rather, the strength of his return to sanity depends in good part upon his recognition that he is fitted by background, intelligence, and sensibility to become the socially responsible person Penrod might have been had he had a conscience, fitted, that is, to become not an all-American boy but what can be called a man.

≡ ACKNOWLEDGMENTS ≡

I thank Gabrielle Dean, Curator of Modern Literary Rare Books and Manuscripts, and Amy Kimball, Head of Materials Management, of the Sheridan Libraries of Johns Hopkins University for their specialist assistance in preparation of this book. Don Jeudes, Librarian for Art History in the Sheridan Libraries, aided in the often complicated arrangement of the illustrations, acting more as collaborator than advisor while bravely suppressing whatever surprise my ignorance may have invoked. I am most grateful for his unflaggingly cheerful assistance. And a very special thanks to Karen Tiefenwerth, who managed all details connected with the preparation and transmission of the manuscript, reducing what I anticipated to be major obstacles to matters of intelligent practice.

≡ NOTES ≡

Chapter One

1. Mason L. Weems, *The Life of Washington*, ed. Marcus Cunliffe (Cambridge, MA: Belknap Press of Harvard University Press, 1962), p. xviii. All quotations are from this edition.

2. Alexis de Tocqueville, *Democracy in America*, trans. George Lawrence (New York: Perennial Classics, 1988), p. 585.

3. See Paul Leicester Ford, "Introduction," *The New England Primer* (New York: Dodd, Mead and Company, 1897), p. 3.

4. *Autobiography*, in *The Portable Benjamin Franklin*, ed. Larzer Ziff (New York: Penguin, 2005), p. 11.

5. William Burlie Brown, *The People's Choice: The Presidential Image in the Campaign Biography* (Baton Rouge: Louisiana State University Press, 1960), p. 43.

6. Nathaniel Hawthorne, *Life of Franklin Pierce* (Boston: Ticknor, Reed, and Fields, 1852), p. 10.

7. *A Small Boy and Others* (Chappaqua, NY: Turtle Point Press, 2001), p. 128.

8. Lysla I. Abbott, "Jacob Abbott: A Goodly Heritage," *Horn Book Magazine* 30 (April 1954): 120.

9. Claude Moore Fuess, *Amherst: The Story of a New England College* (Boston: Little, Brown and Company, 1935), p. 99.

10. Ibid., pp. 100–101.

11. Lysla Abbott, "Jacob Abbott," pp. 125–126.

12. It may be noted in passing that all five Abbott brothers attended Bowdoin and the Andover Seminary and went on to serve in the Congregational ministry, while, in the next generation, all four of Jacob Abbott's sons had distinguished careers in either the church or the law.

13. Lysla Abbott, "Jacob Abbott," pp. 130–131.

14. Liberal theology was also beginning to make its presence felt at Andover. See Daniel Day Williams, *The Andover Liberals: A Study in American Theology* (New York: King's Crown Press, 1941).

15. Lyman Abbott, *Silhouettes of My Contemporaries* (Garden City, NY: Doubleday, Page, & Company, 1921), p. 339.

16. Ibid., p. 341.

Chapter Two

1. Ferris Greenslet, *Thomas Bailey Aldrich* (Boston: Houghton Mifflin Company, 1928), p. 2.

2. F. Marion Crawford, *A Rose of Yesterday* (New York and London: Macmillan, 1897), p. 217.

3. Greenslet, *Thomas Bailey Aldrich*, p. 12.

4. Van Wyck Brooks and Otto L. Bettmann, *Our Literary Heritage* (New York: E. P. Dutton & Company, 1956), p. 177.

5. Greenslet, *Thomas Bailey Aldrich*, p. 20.

6. Brooks and Bettmann, *Our Literary Heritage*, p. 177.

7. Justin Kaplan, *Mr. Clemens and Mark Twain, a Biography* (New York: Simon and Schuster, 1966), p. 144.

8. Greenslet, *Thomas Bailey Aldrich*, p. 81.

9. Marshall B. Davidson et al., *The Writer's America* (New York: American Heritage Publishing Co., 1973), p. 266.

10. William Burlie Brown, *The People's Choice: The Presidential Image in the Campaign Biography* (Baton Rouge: Louisiana State University Press, 1960), p. 43.

11. "Thomas Hughes" in *Oxford Dictionary of National Biography* (Oxford and New York: Oxford University Press, 2004).

12. Alexis de Tocqueville, *Democracy in America*, trans. George Lawrence (New York: Perennial Classics, 1988), p. 584.

13. Joseph E. Kett, *Rites of Passage: Adolescence in America 1790 to the Present* (New York: Basic Books, 1977), pp. 142, 143.

14. "Sperma ceti: *sperma* + *ceti*, gen. Sing. of *cetus*: through an erroneous opinion as to the nature of the substance. Actually a fatty sub-

stance from the head of the whale and to some extent in other parts; it is used primarily in medicinal preparations and the manufacture of candles." *Oxford Universal English Dictionary* (Oxford and New York: Oxford University Press, 2002).

15. Although this magazine had the same name as the one on which Aldrich had once worked, it was a new entity, the former *Saturday Press* having gone out of business in 1860.

16. Ruth Miller Elson, *Guardians of Tradition* (Lincoln: University of Nebraska Press, 1964), pp. 192–193.

17. Kaplan, *Mr. Clemens and Mark Twain*, p. 132.

18. Walter Blair, *Mark Twain & Huck Finn* (Berkeley: University of California Press, 1960), p. 64.

19. Stuart Hutchinson, ed., *Mark Twain, Tom Sawyer and Huckleberry Finn* (New York: Columbia University Press, 1998), pp. 27, 31.

20. Marcia Jacobson, *Being a Boy Again: Autobiography and the American Boy Book* (Tuscaloosa: University of Alabama Press, 1998), pp. 53–54.

21. Hamlin L. Hill, "The Composition and the Structure of *Tom Sawyer*," quoted in Hutchinson, *Mark Twain, Tom Sawyer and Huckleberry Finn*, pp. 19, 21.

22. "Introduction," *The Adventures of Tom Sawyer* (New York: Oxford University Press, 1996), p. xxxviii.

23. Kaplan, *Mr. Clemens and Mark Twain*, p. 383.

24. Blair, *Mark Twain & Huck Finn*, pp. 56–57.

25. Jacobson, *Being a Boy Again*, p. 53, sees Tom and Judge Thatcher as rivals for the possession of Becky.

Chapter Three

1. Allan Nevins, *The Emergence of Modern America, 1865–1878* (New York: Macmillan Company, 1927), pp. 31–33.

2. Charles Loring Brace, *The Dangerous Classes of New York and Twenty Years of Work among Them* (New York: Wynkoop & Hallenbeck, 1872), p. 29.

3. Ibid., p. 23.

4. "Introduction," in *The Portable Benjamin Franklin*, ed. Larzer Ziff (New York: Penguin, 2005).

5. *Ragged Dick, or Street Life in New York*; *Struggling Upward, or Luke Larkin's Luck*; *Jed, the Poorhouse Boy*.

6. See Gary Scharnhorst, "Demythologizing Alger," reprinted in the Norton Critical Edition of Alger's *Ragged Dick*, ed. Hildegard Hoeller (2008). As recently as April 30, 2010, an article in the *New York Times* referred to Lloyd Blankfein, chairman of the board and chief executive officer of Goldman Sachs Group, as a Horatio Alger hero. His father had been a postal clerk.

7. See, for example, "Agriculture and the Farm Problem," Chapter 9 in Samuel Eliot Morison and Henry Commager, *The Growth of the American Republic* (New York: Oxford University Press, 1937).

8. Graduated from Harvard Divinity School, Alger was ordained minister of the Unitarian Society of Brewster, Massachusetts, in 1864. Fifteen months later he resigned after being accused of sexually molesting boys in his congregation. In the entry on Alger in *American National Biography*, Gary Scharnhorst, the foremost authority on his life and writings, says, "there is no record that Alger ever repeated his earlier mistakes."

9. Brace, *Dangerous Classes*, p. 97.

10. The discovery of adolescence, circa 1900, as a distinct stage of human development eroded recapitulation theory.

11. In the first decades of the nineteenth century American schoolbooks classified men by degrees of civilization rather than race. In the later shift to classification by race Indians benefited and were seen as inferior only to whites (Ruth Miller Elson, *Guardians of Tradition* [Lincoln: University of Nebraska Press, 1964], p. 71). Twain, however, appears to have adhered to the earlier textbook beliefs, and in his writings regarded Negroes and Jews, both of whom suffered diminution when race became a factor, with respect and affection, even admiration, while Indians remained uncivilized, untrustworthy, and unlikeable.

12. Charles Dudley Warner, *Being a Boy*, vol. 7 of *Complete Writings* (Hartford, CT: American Publishing Company, 1904), p. 112. The book was first published independently in 1877.

13. William Dean Howells, *A Boy's Town* (New York: Harper & Brothers, 1890), p. 6.

14. Ibid., pp. 210–211.

15. *Democratic Vistas*, in *The Complete Poetry and Prose of Walt Whitman* (New York: Pellegrini & Cudahy, 1948), 2:215.

16. In his *Life* (1855), P. T. Barnum wrote of the early years in which he served in a grocery store where similar practices took place.

17. Quoted in David I. Macleod, *Building Character in the Ameri-*

can Boy: The Boy Scouts, YMCA, and Their Forerunners, 1870–1920 (Madison: University of Wisconsin Press, 1983), p. 54.

18. Ann Thwaites, *Waiting for the Party: The Life of Frances Hodgson Burnett, 1849–1924* (New York: Charles Scribner's Sons, 1974), p. 89.

19. Her novel *Through One Administration* (1883) deals in part with Washington political life.

Chapter Four

1. *Rites of Passage: Adolescence in America 1790 to the Present* (New York: Basic Books, 1977), p. 215.

2. *Complete Writings* (Hartford, CT: American Publishing Company, 1904), vol. 7, p. 9.

3. Ibid., p. 38.

4. *Personal Memoirs of U. S. Grant* (New York: Library of America, n.d.), p. 22.

5. *Boy Life on the Prairie* (New York: Frederick Ungar Publishing Co., 1909), p. 12. First edition was 1899.

6. Ibid., pp. 12–13.

7. Ibid., p. 149.

8. Quoted in John Demos and Virginia Demos, "Adolescence in Historical Perspective," *Journal of Marriage and Family Life* 31 (1969): 635.

9. Kett, *Rites of Passage*, p. 218.

10. "Boy Life in a Massachusetts Country Town Thirty Years Ago," *American Antiquarian Society Proceedings*, n.s. 7 (October 1890–October 1891): 127.

11. *Building Character in the American Boy: The Boy Scouts, YMCA, and Their Forerunners, 1870–1910* (Madison: University of Wisconsin Press, 1983), p. 55.

12. John Levi Cutler, *Gilbert Patten and His Frank Merriwell Saga: A Study in Sub-Literary Fiction, 1896–1913* (Orono, ME: The University Press, 1934), pp. 87–88.

13. "Frank Merriwell's Chums, or Tried and True," 1902.

14. Cutler, *Gilbert Patten*, pp. 7–8.

15. Ibid., p. 65.

16. Ibid., pp. 99, 108.

17. "The Reorientation of American Culture," in *The Origins of*

Modern Consciousness, ed. John Weiss (Detroit: Wayne State University Press, 1965), pp. 27, 32.

18. The marriage of athletics and militaristic patriotism does, however, continue in the parading of the flag by uniformed members of the armed forces, the flyover of air force jets, and the singing of the national anthem at sports events. Concerts, plays, lectures, and other cultural events are not wrapped in similar trappings.

19. E.g., the poetry of Edgar Lee Masters, the stories of Sherwood Anderson, and the novels of Sinclair Lewis.

20. Some series, like the popular radio serial *Henry Aldrich* and the *Andy Hardy* movies, a sequence made up of six films, more than any other series in film history until the arrival of the seventh and eighth films in the *Harry Potter* series, were, to be sure, about adolescents, but the protagonists' family life, comic mistakes, and social awkwardness resembled the pattern *Penrod* had established.

21. Quoted in James Woodress, *Booth Tarkington, Gentleman from Indiana* (Philadelphia: J. B. Lippincott Company, 1954), p. 177.

22. Ibid., pp. 189–190.

23. Ibid., p. 191.

24. Booth Tarkington, *The World Does Move* (Garden City, NY: Doubleday, Doran and Company, 1928), pp. 50, 51.

Chapter Five

1. In the twenty-first century, challenges to the book's suitability for classrooms are addressed to the pervasive use of the word "nigger" by characters who certainly spoke that way at the time and place in which the novel was set, rather than to alleged immoralities of content or claims about disreputable diction, upon which challenges had formerly been based. Neither Ralph Ellison nor Toni Morrison, who have commented on the matter, suffered from such delicacy, and neither do most of the novel's other readers.

2. Victor Fischer, Lin Salamo, and Walter Blair, eds., "Introduction," *Adventures of Huckleberry Finn* (Berkeley: University of California Press, 1988), p. 754.

3. Ibid., p. 763.

4. Ralph Waldo Emerson, *Journals*, ed. E. W. Emerson and W. E. Forbes (London: Constable, 1913), 9:7–8.

5. Fischer, Salamo, and Blair, "Introduction," pp. 759–760.

6. Ibid., pp. 766–767.

7. Eberhard Alsen, *A Reader's Guide to J. D. Salinger* (Westport, CT: Greenwood Press, 2002), p. 54.

8. *In Cold Fear: The Catcher in the Rye, Censorship Controversies and Postwar American Character* (Columbus: Ohio State University Press, 2000), p. 2.

9. "Before he was 17, Sam Clemens had witnessed an aborted lynching of an abolitionist, a death by fire, a hanging, an attempted rape, two drownings, two attempted homicides, and four murders" (Walter Blair, *Mark Twain and Huck Finn* [Berkeley: University of California Press, 1960], p. 55).

10. Gerald Rosen, "A Retrospective Look at *The Catcher in the Rye*," reprinted in *J. D. Salinger*, ed. Harold Bloom (New York: Chelsea House Publishers, 1987), p. 102.

11. Kenneth Slawenski, *J. D. Salinger: A Life* (New York: Random House, 2010), p. 102n.

12. Ibid., p. 215.

≡ INDEX ≡